Sail Fitter

**Sailing Fitness and Training
Second Edition**

Michael Blackburn, BApSc (Hons), PhD

Sail Fitter
© 2001 by Michael Blackburn

First edition (Sail Fit) published 1997

Published by Fitness Books
8/25 Parkes St, Manly Vale NSW 2093, Australia.
1michaelblackburn@compuserve.com

ISBN 0-9578805-0-2

Photos: Cover - Belinda Stowell and Jenny Armstrong 470 Gold Medallists, by A. Wheeler.
All other photos by Bob Ross, V. Kovalenko, B. Stowell, J. Kelly and M. Blackburn; p97 by Andrea Francolini.

Printed by Southwood Press

CONTENTS

Foreword	v
Introduction	vii
1. Food, Drink, Exercise and Body Weight	**1**
▶ Body Weight	1
▶ Changing Body Mass	1
▶ Nutrition - Fast Foods	5
▶ Sports Drinks	10
2. Physical Fitness	**14**
▶ Getting Fit and Keeping Fit - Basics of Sailing Fitness Training	14
▶ What should I do in the Gym?	16
3. Training for Hiking - no Walk in the Park	**17**
▶ Research on Hiking	17
▶ Key Findings	18
▶ What the Results Mean for You	20
▶ Advanced Hiking Technique	22
4. Trapezing Fitness	**26**
▶ The Harness	26
▶ Donning the Nappy	27
▶ Trapezing Technique	27
▶ Tacking	28
▶ Advanced techniques	29
5. Sailboarding Fitness	**31**
6. How to Spend Your Sailing Time	**33**
7. Top Seven Training Sessions	**35**
▶ No.7 – Postural/hiking muscles: Crunch and reverse sit-ups	35
▶ No.6 – Hiking and sheeting endurance: Wall-sit and body pull up	36
▶ No.5 – Muscle Strength: Weight training	36
▶ No.4 – Endurance: Exercise bike and rowing machine	38
▶ No.3 – Endurance: Cycling	39
▶ No.2 – The Simulator: Hiking bench and land boat training	40
▶ No.1 – Sailing	41
▶ Top 7 Session Summary	45
8. Yearly Training	**46**
▶ Background Training	46
▶ Work 1	47
▶ Peak 1	48
▶ Work 2	51
▶ Peak 2	51
▶ Transition Phase	52
9. Recovery - Revive and Survive	**55**
10. Eight-Week Training Program	**59**
▶ Notes on the Program	59
▶ Sample Training Program	60
11. Home Fitness Test	**61**
▶ Body Weight	61

- ▶ Flexibility - Sit and Reach Test — 61
- ▶ Abdominal Endurance — 62
- ▶ Body-weight Pull-ups — 62
- ▶ Wall-sit — 63
- ▶ Practical Aerobic Test – Personal Time Trial — 63

12. Avoiding injury — 64
- ▶ Eyes — 64
- ▶ Skin - Sun — 65
- ▶ Foreign Bodies — 65
- ▶ Cuts and Abrasions — 66
- ▶ Fitness and Avoiding Injury — 67

13. Dressed for Success - Sailing Clothing — 69
- ▶ Keeping Warm When it's Cool — 69
- ▶ Don't Get Beat Up — 70
- ▶ Be Cool when it's Hot and Wet — 72
- ▶ The Personal Flotation Device — 74

14. Lower Backs - The Stayed Back — 75
- ▶ Hiking Muscles — 75
- ▶ Preventing Back Pain — 77

15. Travelling in a Jet Plane — 80
- ▶ Jet Lag — 80
- ▶ Jet Stress — 80
- ▶ Avoiding sickness — 81

16. Fitness for Young Sailors — 82
- ▶ Comments — 84

17. Fitness for Masters Sailors and Old Salts — 86
- ▶ Comments — 88

18. Lifestyle Factors — 89

19. On-Water Training — 91
- ▶ Training Drills — 91
- ▶ Sample On Water Training Session — 99

20. "Like Riding a Bike" - Sailing Skills — 102
- ▶ Cue Words — 102
- ▶ Breaking Down Skills — 102
- ▶ Practice — 103
- ▶ Highly Skilled? — 103
- ▶ Too Similar Skills — 103

Finally — 104

Sailing Library — 105

Appendix: Gym exercises — 106
- Abdominal — 106
- Chest and Triceps — 110
- Legs — 111
- Upper Back & Biceps — 112
- Lower Back — 115
- Shoulders — 116
- Abdominal Stability — 117

▶▶FOREWORD

I could not think of anyone better qualified to write a book about fitness for small boat sailing than Michael Blackburn. He's academically qualified, with a PhD degree in Sports Science. He can sail well, at the top international level, with a Bronze medal from the Sydney 2000 Games marking the end of two Olympic campaigns in the Laser class before embarking on a new Olympic challenge, sailing with Chris Nicholson in the exciting 49er skiff.

And, from the informative articles on fitness and small-boat sailing techniques he has written for *Australian Sailing* magazine, I know that he can write clearly on sometimes quite complex physiological and racing topics.

While the first edition of *Sail Fitness and Training* was certainly a compulsory acquisition for any Laser sailor who wanted to be more competitive, this second edition has broadened in outlook as Michael himself moves onto the somewhat different physical requirements of becoming an agile, as well as strong, 49er crew.

It is enhanced, too, by the experiences from Michael's dogged physical and mental campaigning and planning for the Sydney Olympics. It still tells you how Michael Blackburn developed from the scrawny 68kg teenager I first watched racing Laser Radials to the 30-year-old muscular Olympian, with advice on eating, drinking and exercising to change body mass and gain or lose weight.

To the advice on gym work and programming has been added specifics on weight training with full photographic illustration of all the recommended exercises.

The completely new topics in the second edition include clothing and PFDs, fitness for sailboarders, fitness and techniques for trapezing crews. Fitness for young sailors (aged 9-16) and for masters sailors and 'old salts' is included for the first time with case studies for each that help make the advice for each age group personally relevant.

The pre-Olympic campaign experience, woven throughout the book, yields also some advice on battling jet lag and jet stress that all long-distance travellers would find useful.

You do not need to be an Olympic aspirant or a gym "junkie" to benefit from reading *Sail Fitter*. As its concluding paragraph says: "The exercises and ideas in this book are not just for seriously competitive sailors. You may sail mostly in local competition and go to a bigger regatta once a year to see where you're at; you'll be better than last year if you're fitter and can handle the boat well. The reassurance you get from sailing better will, I hope, help you achieve whatever your goals may be."

Bob Ross, Editor, *Australian Sailing* magazine.

▶▶INTRODUCTION

I entered my first big open-water Laser regatta – the Asian-Pacific titles back in 1990. We had five days of 20 to 25 knot winds and triple world champ Glenn Bourke, at his fittest, was loving it, winning five of the long-course races in a row. Back in the fleet I battled it out with others my size (around 70 kg) and level of fitness, finishing 41st overall.

My fitness and body weight have improved a lot since then and I have gone on to finish in the top three in a number of World or Olympic level regattas. However, it took a number of years of good training to be fit enough to match it with the stars of Laser sailing – dual Olympic medallists Ben Ainslie and Robert Scheidt. This is because the fastest techniques in small boat sailing are tough to do: The trunk is leant back further and thrown forward and/or backwards in response to *every* wave; the sail is trimmed almost as regularly to keep it at the optimum angle to the wind and every chance to surf the boat down a wave is leapt upon.

You can get fitter too. Greater sailing fitness comes from:
- Doing training that is specific to the sport
- Progressively increasing the volume (hours) and intensity (how hard) of exercise
- Avoiding injury
- Eating well
- Getting enough rest when you need it.

In all but the lightest winds, better fitness – including flexibility, endurance, strength and agility – will make it easier to execute skills like hiking, tacking, gybing and sailing upwind and get you around the course faster. This completely revised and updated edition, *Sail Fitter*, is the how-to guide to improving your fitness for sailing.

This book doesn't cover sailing tactics and strategy – other books cover these areas well. Instead, the focus is on the body and physical factors that can affect performance. Compared to the previous edition, *Sail Fit*, this book has been revised and updated throughout. Many new topics have been added, for example, youth and masters sailing, gym exercises, clothing, and fitness for trapezing crews and sailboarders.

As with all exercise programs, you should take care when starting and seek medical advice first if you're a real couch potato. A number of exercises in the book are very demanding and should not be attempted without significant background training.

Finally, thank you to the reviewers of this second edition, especially my mum, for her support over many years and offering valuable insights. I also greatly appreciate the help of Bob Ross, editor of *Australian Sailing* magazine who supplied many of the action photos.

Good sailing,
Michael Blackburn.

▶▶1. FOOD, DRINK, EXERCISE AND BODY WEIGHT

▶Body Weight

Achieving the right body weight for your class eliminates one of the basic excuses in sailing! Suggested body weights for Olympic and small boat classes are given in the table below. If you are much lighter in body weight than recommended, heavy-weather performance will be predictably poor, however good a sailor you are. If you are much heavier, downwind and lighter wind performance will suffer. Superior fitness in the muscles used for hiking and sheeting allows a slightly lighter crew to have an advantage on downwind legs.

Guideline optimal weights (kg) for sailors of Olympic and Laser Radial classes.

Class	Skipper	Crew	Total	2000 Olympic Medallists' average
470 men	60-65	67-74	130-138	137 (63/71)*
470 women	52-60	64-70	117-130	119 (58/66)*
49er	70-75	76-80	146-155	153 (74/79)*
Europe	63-70			69
Finn	95-110			102
Laser	78-83			80
Laser Radial	65-72			n/a
Mistral men	65-70			68
Mistral women	52-59			56
Tornado	70-75	70-80	140-150	149
Yngling	TBA			n/a

*(Skipper/crew)

It's also a good idea to check what your all-up sailing weight is, fully clothed – boots, jumpers, wetsuit, etc. Hop on a set of scales when you get off the water all wet. While my body weight is around 80kg, my sailing weight could be up to 86-87kg.

To adjust your body weight to the optimal, you need good exercise and nutrition. For instance, if you like Laser sailing and want a shot at the Olympics, you may start as 68 kg weakling teenager and struggle for many years to put on weight, but regular training will certainly pay off. It took me three years of serious eating and weight training to grow from around 70 kg to around 80 kg while adding little fat. For many people it's possible to reach the weight needed for your chosen class but it will take considerable commitment if you naturally fall outside the ideal range.

▶Changing Body Mass

Your body's weight depends on your energy balance. This is the difference between energy in and energy out. Energy in is food and drink (kilojoules). Energy out is in two parts: There is the essential metabolism which is the energy needed to simply run the functions of the body – digestion, breathing, heart beat and so on. This can amount to around 50 to 70 per cent of the total. The more muscle and less fat on a body, the faster the basic metabolism. Then there is exercise which consumes energy above the resting level. The energy used here is proportional to the intensity and duration of activity. For active people as much as 50 per cent of daily energy expenditure goes on working the muscles and energy supply systems.

- ## Gaining Weight

To gain weight, energy in needs to be greater than energy out. Basically, eat more and start weight training using heavy weights, with 6 – 10 repetitions to failure. Failure in doing say, eight repetitions, is when you can only *just* complete the eight, with good technique, and not be able to lift the weight again. A weight-training partner may be needed with some exercises involving free weights (barbells and dumbbells) to help you lift the last repetition successfully. A sample weight training program and exercises are given later.

Make sure to include exercises involving large muscle groups – thigh and bottom – in your gym program. A 10 per cent increase in the size of these muscle groups will entail a greater gain in body mass than a 10 per cent increase in size of smaller groups of muscles. If you are under 16 years of age it's probably better not to use heavy dumbbells and barbells, rather, your own body weight can be used as resistance (e.g., chin-ups and push ups). Other suitable exercises for youths can be devised using 8 – 12 mm shock-cord (e.g., to replicate the sheeting action).

If you are not engaged in an exercise program, the gain in weight from extra eating will be mainly in stored fat. If you follow an exercise program while you're eating more, the weight gain will be mainly lean weight, especially muscle. The latter is, of course, far better.

For many people, gaining weight is easy – especially in the form of fat. However, highly active individuals often have trouble gaining weight. Here are some tips:

- Eat four to five quality 'meals' a day – aim to never feel really hungry. Sometimes you may have to sit down and eat when you feel full.

- Ensure the food is rich in carbohydrates (60 to 80 per cent rice, pasta, cereals, fruit); protein (20 per cent lean meats, eggs, fish) and fats (20 per cent butter, margarine, nuts, cheese) will make up the rest. Aim for carbohydrates *lower* in fibre (read the nutrition labels) since raw fibre is not absorbed by the body; for example, use white bread and more processed breakfast cereals like Rice Bubbles and Corn Flakes rather than Weet-Bix and Sultana Bran. Note that fibre is a necessary part of a healthy diet to keep you regular. Nonetheless, making your diet lower in fibre should not be a problem when you are eating a lot of food since there will be enough fibre in the total volume of food eaten.

- You may need to cut down on long duration, energy-sapping endurance exercise (e.g., running and cycling) in favour of weights in the gym. My weight gain program included three sessions per week of heavy weights sessions (about three-quarters to one hour each) and just one or two bike rides per week (about one hour each) apart from the on-water training.

- Take some of your foods in liquid form. Sprint legend Carl Lewis regularly used a blender or juicer to liquefy fruits and vegetables so that the foods were absorbed more easily and faster.

Liquid booster:
Into a blender toss 400ml milk, 2 tablespoons of Sustagen (a carbohydrate and protein powder), 2 scoops of low-fat ice cream, 1 egg (optional) and blend for 30 sec. Enjoy.

Muscle will contribute far more to your performance than fat, so putting on muscle is definitely better. Since getting fatter by eating the wrong foods is the unhealthy option and will not help you train well, also look at whether wearing more clothing on the water is an option.

When a training program is started, the body uses extra energy to build the necessary tissues and muscles as well as secrete enzymes and hormones. If you are a thin person you may therefore have to eat a high volume of food to gain weight. If you do this, you may in fact lose weight at first but keep at it – the body is starting to become a finely tuned machine.

Before jumping into a class of boat know that there is an ideal height and body weight range for each. You basically got your height from your parents, but you can adjust your body weight to some extent to suit your chosen class.

• Losing Weight

To lose weight, energy out has to be greater than energy in. Usually, the process involves a loss of fat with a slight gain in muscle or lean tissue. This speeds up basal metabolism to help further loss or maintenance of the target weight. Moderately paced endurance exercise – 30 minutes or more five times a week – is the best exercise for building up your fat-burning ability. Cycling, running, swimming and windy-weather sailing are ideal. To develop strength at the same time, lighter weights can be lifted in the gym with higher repetitions (e.g., 12 to 25 repetitions).

In terms of food, avoid fat. Second, avoid fat. Third, ... By cutting the fat intake, carbohydrate-rich foods naturally make up the bulk of the intake. This is also great for improving your endurance in training and competition.

A loss of approximately one kilogram a week is considered the maximum safe rate of weight loss. However, extremely active people, because of their high-energy expenditures, or extremely obese people, due to their sheer bulk and energy needed to move their bodies, may lose weight a little faster.

Weigh yourself on the most accurate scales you can find – don't expect reliability from cheaper bathroom scales. Note that your body weight can easily change by 1-2% in a day. It's usually highest after your evening meal and lowest in the morning, after going to the bathroom. So, if you need to keep track of your weight, measure it at a set time of day.

Body fat won't be shaken, rocked, knocked or baked off. The only way is to eat less fat and exercise more. Thereby, you'll keep your muscles while losing spare flesh.

Once the target weight is reached your nutrition remains important to make sure you get the carbohydrates, proteins, fats, vitamins, minerals and so on to perform your best. Read on for information on a 'training diet'.

▶ Nutrition – Fast Foods
• Training Diet

Nutritionists often say we need to eat more complex carbohydrates like breads, cereals, fruit, vegies, etc., and less fat, salt and sugary foods. Eating less fat means eating more vitamins, minerals, energy and protein which helps you meet your nutritional goals.

Check out the 'nutritional information' table on the packaged foods you buy. The value quoted for 'Fat (per 100g/ml)' tells all. The golden rule is mostly eat foods 5g fat/100g or less. Avoid foods with more than 10g fat per 100g. Fat in unpackaged foods or those without a nutritional table is harder to spot. For these, choose foods with no visible fat (the white spots in salami are mostly fat) or look at the ingredient list. The higher in the ingredient list, the more of that ingredient in the food. Therefore, if 'vegetable fats and oils', 'cheddar cheese' or 'chocolate' are listed early on you know to avoid the food because it contains a large percentage of fat.

Nutrition label from a breakfast cereal.

	Nutritional Information	
	Per 45g serve	Per 100g
Energy	720 kJ	1596 kJ
Protein	3.9 g	8.7 g
Fat	1.9 g	2.8 g
Carbohydrate		
- Total	34.6 g	80.1 g
- Sugars	7.5 g	16.8 g
Dietary Fibre	3.1 g	6.0 g
Cholesterol	0 mg	0 mg
Sodium	98 mg	205 mg
Potassium	165 mg	357 mg
Niacin	2.4 mg	5.6 mg
Vitamin C	10.0 mg	22.2 mg
Folate	100.0 µg	222.2 µg
Iron	3.0 mg	6.7 mg

Some nutrients go well together: Vitamin C-rich foods (eg, oranges) enhance iron absorption (eg, from meat) when eaten in the same meal.

However, the iron in spinach is not as easily taken up by the body as that found in meat.

The more fibre in a meal the greater chance that the fibre will carry the other nutrients contained in the meal right through the digestive tract and out the other end before they can be absorbed.

When the level of fat in your diet is down, you should find yourself hungrier during the day. This is fine, just eat more of the same low-fat food. Carbohydrates – rice, pasta, bread, fruits, cereals – are less dense in energy than fats, so the volume of food which is eaten on a low-fat diet is large. Elite athletes often have five or more meals a day when training as their bodies' carbohydrate stores are continually being demolished by heavy workouts.

Usually there is no need for vitamin, mineral or other pills to supplement food intake. However, people who have a low overall food intake (including those wanting to lose weight) need to choose foods carefully all the time to keep the body stocked-up on nutrients like iron, and the B-vitamins.

• Pre-Race Nutrition

Carbohydrate loading, where you deplete (by exercising) and then stuff yourself with carbohydrates in the days before an event, works well for endurance athletes. However, the types of full carbo-loading plans which cyclists and runners follow for up to a week before an important event are cumbersome for sailors – we don't even know when the first windy race of the regatta will be and when the energy is needed.

For sailors, modified carbo-loading, which involves bumping up carbo intake (70 to 85 per cent of calories) in the two to three days prior to competition while tapering training and not exercising the day before the event, can be used as an effective alternative. This may mean missing an invitation race and just having a short sail two days before the first race.

Simple pre-regatta activity and nutritional plan

Days to Go	Activity
4	Quality sailing and normal diet
3	Longer sail and extra-high carbohydrates
2	High quality, shorter sail and extra-high carbos
1	Rest
0	Race

It is important to eat before a race. This may be only an hour or two before going on the water, for instance, just before you rig the boat. Then, the food will be cleared from the stomach before the start of the race. In terms of what to eat, this is one time when a balanced meal isn't as important – the food needs to be mainly carbohydrates – bananas, bread, cereals, pasta, rice, fruit juices, low fat milk or yoghurt are all appropriate. Remember that fatty foods (hot chips, pies and chocolate bars) are neither needed nor desirable within the four hours prior to, during or after exercise.

It's important to find a good source of quality food at regattas, whether eating at home or out.

The only time carbohydrate intake (and all food in fact) may not be appropriate is during the 10 to 60 minutes prior to a race. This is because the body will start to digest the food before the race starts, taking blood away from your muscles during the race. This digestion process will also involve a drop in blood glucose levels that can create physical and mental sluggishness.

• Eating on the Water

During a windy race, drinking carbohydrates can improve your physical performance by updating energy stores. While the effectiveness of carbos is hard to measure in sailing performance there is no doubt that it extends runners' and cyclists' endurance so the likely advantage to sailors is worth chasing. Liquid carbohydrates are probably better than solids since at the same time you achieve the goals of carbohydrate and fluid intake. Weak cordial, fruit juices, and most sports drinks (such as Isosport, Gatorade, Sportplus, PowerAde) are all better than plain water when you have to spend a number of hours on the water. Again, pick the one you like best. Drink small amounts regularly, such as on each downwind leg of the course. More about sports drinks later.

• Between Races

In approximate order of speed of removal from the stomach (fastest to slowest): moderately concentrated sports drink, water, heavily concentrated carbohydrate drink, alcohol, semi-solid carbohydrate food, solid carbohydrate, mainly protein food, mainly fat/fibre food.

If you have a short on-water break between races you still have to be wary of eating the wrong type of food or of eating too much. Common snacks like Coke and Mars bars are inappropriate. The fizzy Coke also contains caffeine that promotes water loss from the body while the Mars bar is too high in fat and clogs the stomach. Taking in a sports drink will always be safe – 500mls is probably a suitable amount to drink in a 30 minute break between races. Solid foods can be fine too. Bananas are an easily digestible carbohydrate along with other fruits, sultanas and low-fat food bars, such as Power Bars. It is good to wash solid foods down with a drink to aid digestion and for re-hydration.

No, not a good pre- or between-race drink – but handy for launching a new boat!

• Post-Race Nutrition

Grilled or baked potato chips are fine. Deep-fried chips will have absorbed too much fat.

Post-training or post-race nutrition is usually neglected in the need to pack the boat up, get showered and changed and into something more warm and comfortable, like a bucket of hot chips! However, during a regatta, it is important to refuel with carbos and replenish your muscles' energy stores as soon as possible after a windy race.

Research has shown that if carbohydrate is not eaten during the first two hours after heavy endurance exercise, your body's muscle energy stores will have trouble returning to normal levels in 24 hours (i.e., in time for the following day's race). Keep eating mainly carbos – whether grazing or in a meal – for up to six hours after a heavy race as the body may still be starving for them at this stage.

Fast recipe:
Egg bread – Crack one egg into a bowl and lightly cover with breadcrumbs. Mix, adding more crumbs until you can just roll the lot into a ball by hand. Flatten and grill until golden brown. You can mix in other ingredients to taste.
This is a high-protein, high-carbohydrate, low fat part of dinner.

The equivalent of say, two to three bananas or something else easily broken down by the body, including certain sports drinks (500mls+) and sugar-based snack foods, are very appropriate when you hit the shore. This is a time when snacking on jellybeans and snakes is highly recommended! Personally, I like to take in some carbohydrate polymer that comes in small sachets and I carry in my life jacket (available at sports and cycle shops). Soon after finishing, I take in 50g of pure carbohydrate to accelerate recovery.

Liquid supplements such as Lucozade or Exceed are also good post-race because they are easy to digest, less filling than solids and provide a source of fluid for re-hydration. You should experiment with any new pre- and post-exercise eating practice during club races. Then, you will become aware of your body's reaction to particular types of carbohydrates, as each individual's metabolism is different.

I've stressed the use of carbohydrates for better performance, taken prior to and during competition, but they are also an important part of the everyday diet, whether training or not. In fact, the elite athlete's diet is not much different to that recommended for everyone else.

Good nutrition doesn't mean being overly strict about all things that pass your lips. Even the best endurance athletes will eat 15 per cent junk food but 85 per cent of the time stick to a nutritious low-fat diet for training and serious competitions.

Fast Food/Fat Check List	
IN (fast food): Always eat, except 10-60 min before exercise	OUT (slow food): Avoid eating regularly
breads	full-fat cheese
cereals	chocolate bars
dried fruit	hot chips
fruits & vegies	donuts
fruit juices	Mac-burgers
low-fat milk/yoghurt	margarine/butter
rice	pies
sports drinks	sausage rolls

Food preparation. An important but often forgotten factor in nutrition is what happens to a food's nutritional value during its preparation. You may think that boiling up and eating a portion of carrots and peas would mean that you're getting a good whack of vitamins. However, you may be better off drinking the water you boil these vegetables in because up to half of the water-soluble vitamins – thiamine, riboflavin and Vitamin C plus minerals – would have leaked out. Losses are related to how much the food has been cut up, the amount and length of time in the water.

One of the best ways to eat fruit and vegetables is raw. Vegetables cooked from frozen usually offer better nutrition than the same food canned. Steam the vegetables over water or in a microwave rather than boil them in water and otherwise prepare fruit and vegetables as little as possible before eating.

Processed foods. In general, food processing involves a trade-off between making the food safer and giving it a longer life, but often at the cost of lowered vitamin and mineral content.

Fast recipe: eggana drink– Into a blender put milk, low-fat ice cream, an egg and a banana and blend. Another low fat and nutrient-rich drink.

Some processed foods are denser in nutrients, and some less, than their unprocessed counterparts. Foods such as potato chips are heavily processed; they have been subjected to excessive heat treatment, alteration of form, and addition of fat and salt; and they have lost nutrients and gained kilojoules along the way.

Fortified pasteurised non-fat milk is also a processed food, but it has been minimally heat-treated, has gained nutrients and has lost kilojoules.

Potato chips are nutritionally inferior to potatoes, then, but fortified non-fat milk is nutritionally superior to whole milk for people whose energy intakes limit their nutrient intakes. So, it's not whether a food is processed or unprocessed, but how it is processed that determines its nutritional value.

Eating away from home. Away from home it's often more of a challenge to get the food you are used to. For practical and financial reasons, I recommend 'shopping' from your own cupboard at home before leaving. Then you can gather together small, long-life products like spreads, rice, pasta and fruit bars. For overseas competitions it's also good to take a small volume of harder to get items, like your favourite snack foods and sports drinks.

▶ Sports Drinks

During a windy race, drinking carbohydrate-based drinks such as Gatorade can improve your physical performance by topping up the muscles' energy stores. As mentioned, liquid carbohydrates are probably better than solids during a race as they allow you to achieve the goals of carbohydrate and fluid intake at the same time.

Drinking is a must before, during and after activity to keep the blood volume topped up and avoid dehydration. This helps maintain your heart rate and body temperature at good levels. Sports drinks have been developed to maximise fluid replacement and are convenient. But which drink? Do the electrolytes in Staminade make it better than Gatorade? What about the newer Powerade and age-old Lucozade? (Why do they all end in 'ade'?) Will plain cordial or fruit juice – often at half the price of 'sports drinks' – do the same job? And what of the claims of Exceed, Isosport, Sportsplus and Sustagen and all the others?

Gatorade and other sports drinks offer many cool flavours.

The confusion about sports drinks is lessened if the types are understood. There are three types: fluid replacers, carbohydrate loaders, and nutrient supplements. What you need to consider when choosing a drink are when you intend to use it and the type of activity.

• Carbohydrate Loaders

Drink carbohydrate loaders such as Lucozade well before or after exercise. They contain more than 10 per cent carbohydrate which means relatively slow absorption from the stomach. On the plus side they can help maximise the body's energy stores and provide a strong hit of carbohydrate. This can help the body load-up in the days before an event as well as put back much of the lost energy while the body is recovering after exercise.

• Fluid Replacers

Since a fluid-replacing drink is taken during exercise, it should have less carbohydrate – five to eight per cent – to avoid clogging up the stomach and ensure the body gets the water and energy it needs. These are the more common types of 'sports' drinks on the market and include Isostar, Gatorade and Powerade. They differ little in their actual energy content (i.e., the kilojoules in each), although the type of carbohydrate (sugar) you read on the label often differs between sucrose, fructose, glucose and glucose polymer.

A drink based on glucose may be absorbed too quickly and negatively affect insulin levels and the amount of glucose in the blood (for instance, Staminade has glucose in a four per cent solution). This can cause mental and physical lethargy not welcome during a race. Better at this stage is a drink with glucose polymer or fructose which is absorbed more evenly (e.g., Exceed has glucose polymer and fructose in a 7.5 per cent solution).

Note that cooler drinks (10 to 15°C) are absorbed faster than warmer fluids. This gets the energy in faster and also helps to cool the body on a warm day. Unfortunately, 'room temperature' drinks are inevitable on most racing boats to save on the space and weight of a cooler.

Weak cordial offers a low-budget and tasty alternative as a during-race drink. Cordial, fruit juices, and most sports drinks help to top-up carbohydrate levels during a long day on the water. Pick the one you like best and remember to drink small amounts regularly while racing, such as on each leg of the course – as a guide, 150mls every 15 to 20 minutes.

- **Nutrient Supplements**

The third type of sports drink, a nutrient supplement drink, contains the sort of vitamins, minerals, protein and energy you get in normal food but in a fluid which may be digested quicker. These are used well apart from exercise and may be useful when training hard to ensure the body gets adequate nutrition. Otherwise, they are usually not needed to maintain good health and are generally more expensive than eating foods with similar levels of vitamins, protein and minerals.

See the drinks summary table for a quick comparison between the major sports drinks.

Sports Drinks Summary

Sports Drinks: Types Examples	Energy (kJ / 100g)	Main Uses
Carbohydrate Loaders	Moderate	Boosts carbohydrate stores before or after sailing.
Exceed high carbohydrate source	425	
Lucozade	309	
Solid foods (e.g., cereals and rice)	Moderate - high	
Fluid Replacers	Low	Important while sailing for energy and re-hydration.
Cottee's cordial (approx.)	127	
Exceed Fluid and Energy Replacement	117	
Gatorade	120	
Isosport	121	
Isostar	116	
Powerade	134	
Sports Plus	120	
Nutrient Supplements	High	Adds to kilojoule and nutrient intake.
Exceed Sports Nutrition Supplement	1365	
Sustagen Sport	1490	
Many body-building compounds	High	

▶▶2. PHYSICAL FITNESS

▶Getting Fit and Keeping Fit – Basics of Sailing Fitness Training

Principles of training:
1. Overload - to gain fitness, undertake a training load exceeding that to which you are accustomed.

2. Recovery - the body must be allowed to repair and regenerate before the next training load.

3. Reversibility - if training ceases, your body will return to its initial level of fitness - if you don't use it you will lose it!

4. Specificity - you will get maximum benefit from your training when it replicates the movements and energy requirements involved in the sport.

5. Individuality - different athletes have different training needs and preferences and will respond in varying fashions to a training program.

Many competitive small boat sailors get involved in different sorts of physical exercise during the week and this helps them make sure their legs and arms don't let their minds down for windy weekend races. But few sailors can claim that their weekday exercise routine is the absolute best they can get to improve their fitness for sailing.

Between 50 and 70 per cent of the average windy race is spent trying to hike or trapeze the boat flat going upwind. Or, in the case of sailboarding, frequent pumping is vital to keep average speed up. The discomfort inherent in these activities can be reduced by regularly doing work-outs that are specific to our sport, that is, focusing on the thighs, hips, abdomen, lower back and arms. While running, aerobics or swimming may be appropriate for keeping the heart and circulation in shape, physiologically these exercises don't relate well enough to small boat sailing to be the focus your training program. In fact, you can do serious damage to parts of your body if you haven't developed the right muscles for sailing.

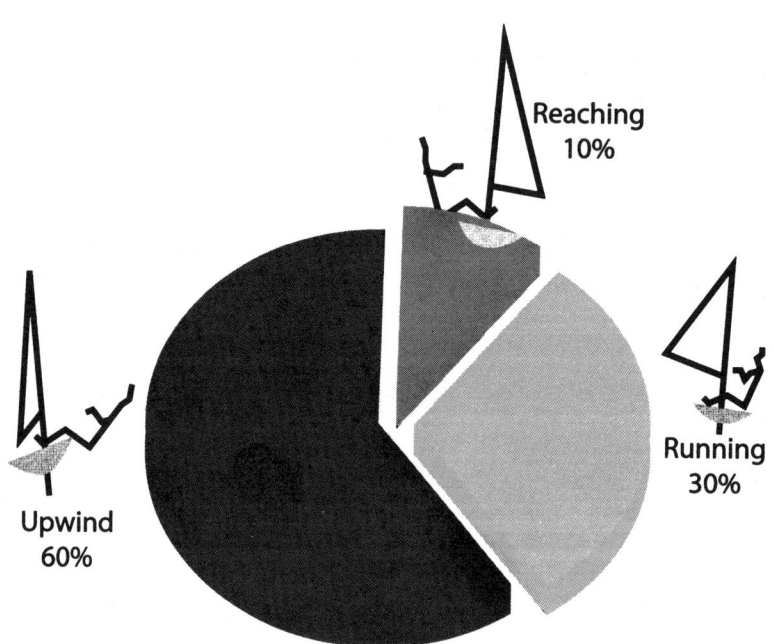

Time in Motion: Olympic class races are set to last about 60 minutes, except 49ers and Mistrals which have races about 30 minutes long.

Aerobics is good training for aerobics, running is good training for running, swimming for swimming, and so on, but really we must sail to physically train for sailing – so get out on the water!

However, most of us can't or don't sail often enough to improve our sailing fitness. Therefore, we need appropriate exercises to develop our fitness between weekend events and regattas. Training in other sports and activities will be useful if they work the body in a similar way to sailing. Consider this – after an aerobics class, would you feel fatigued *in the same way* as when you finish a sailing race? You won't, because during aerobics the muscles and cardiovascular system are stressed in a different way to sailing. Therefore, the benefit to your sailing fitness will not be great.

Only exercises that are highly compatible with the demands of sailing will improve sailing fitness. Imagine world-class hockey players spending most of their off-field training time swimming laps. They simply wouldn't. But this is akin to what many sailors are doing by going to aerobics and jogging as their only fitness training for sailing.

The rough value of other exercises for small boat sailing fitness is illustrated on the figure – the higher the points, the more specific and beneficial the exercise is to your sailing fitness. The exercises are rated on the basis of their relevance to sailing in terms of muscle involvement (thigh muscles for hiking, arm and shoulder muscles for sheeting), type of muscle contraction (mostly static contractions in hiking and sheeting) and the extent to which the muscular effort is continuous (almost non-stop in hiking and sheeting). Choose activities higher on the list to improve your fitness for sailing.

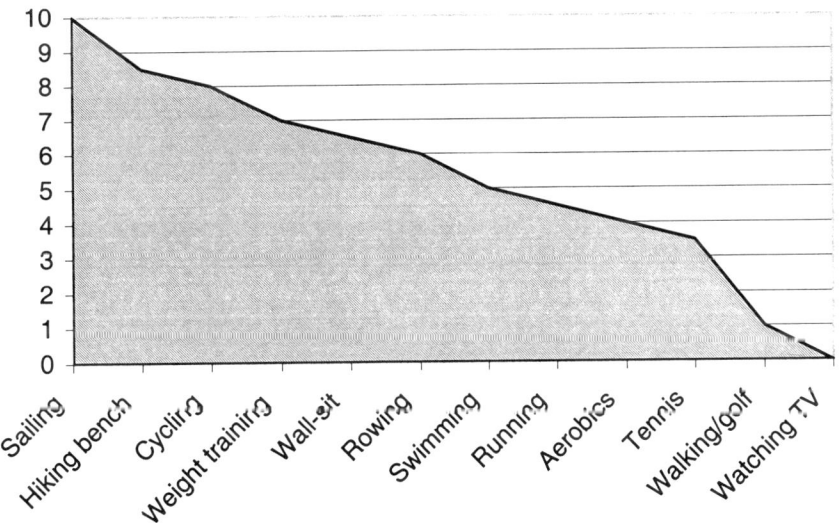

The bonus from sport-specific training: Rating out of ten for different sports and exercises to physically train for small boat sailing.

Training variables:
1. Intensity - heart rate is a good, simple and accurate indicator of exercise intensity. Roughly, you will need to work in a heart rate range of 120-160 beats per minute to make gains in aerobic fitness. To increase your strength, say, to lift your boat, your muscles will need to do repeated short, hard efforts, with a suitable rest afterwards.

2. Duration - you need to work over a long enough period (30+ min) to improve your aerobic fitness and strength. Typically an aerobic workout would be more continuous in activity than the strength session. A really long session (2-4 hrs) is ok if you are fit enough to handle it, but it may mean you will need more rest before the next session.

3. Frequency - How often. Three training sessions per week is usually regarded as the minimum to make steady gains in aerobic fitness or your muscle's strength. Top Olympic sailors do 8-12 different sessions per week.

4. Volume - When you multiply frequency by duration you get volume. It's usually measured per week. Minimum volume would be about two hours per week. Maximum volume depends on your fitness, but lets say that 20-25 hours is a lot!

Cycling, hiking benches, rowing, weight training and the simple wall-sit (propping yourself against a wall with legs bent) all give the thighs a solid work-out and with consistent training will help to improve the muscles' endurance while hiking. Focus on these activities to hike longer and stronger during a race.

During a week you should aim to do over 35 points worth. This could be made up of: one windy weekend race (10 points) one bike ride (45 minutes) at 8 points, two weight training sessions (40 to 45 minutes, 14 points) and leaning from a hiking bench (30 minutes, 8.5 points). The more specific the activity, the more efficient your training! Full-time small boat sailors would do 70-100 points worth a week!

Note that the occasional training session in one of the lesser-ranked activities is not all bad since they impose different stresses and strains on the body. This gives the body a welcome change and may help suppress the development of overuse injuries from doing the same training all the time.

Swimming is notable in this context since it's an activity where injuries are less common and more or less, it gives a whole-body work-out. Also, its value for sailing fitness can be boosted by putting flippers on the feet and doing laps of kicking only. Your flippers should be a good size and fairly stiff, to add to the power you can get while kicking. They will exaggerate the work done by the thigh, hip, buttock and ankle muscles that are important in hiking.

▶What should I do in the Gym?

The above illustrates a little about what type of exercise is best but I often get asked 'What should I do in the gym?' The type of exercise you do in a gym is only one of the variables that are important in a training program. Apart from doing specific exercise, the other important factors to consider are the intensity, duration, frequency and volume of exercise. The body will grow in its fitness according to how you manipulate these factors in training. Importantly, the overriding principle of specificity remains – train as you sail.

▶▶3. Training for Hiking – no Walk in the Park

At least since the 1950s, small boat sailors, including the legendary Paul Elvstrom, had cloth straps along the centre-line of their boats. The feet were hooked under these straps, so that the whole trunk could be held beyond the edge of the boat. This addition dramatically improved the speed of sailing dinghies in strong winds because a far greater righting moment could be exerted by the body to balance the wind's heeling force. This leaning out over the side of the boat is known as hiking – the most dreaded activity in small boat sailing!

There is a definite limit to how long small boat sailors can hold an effective hiking position. Felt your legs start to burn even before the end of the first beat? Hiking involves static contractions of the large muscles of the thighs and trunk. Static contractions involve a muscle developing tension without making the joints move. These contractions are dominant in small boat sailing – another example is holding the mainsheet.

Even at relatively low levels of static muscle tension, the blood vessels can be squeezed shut and the ensuing lack of blood flow and oxygen to the muscles will rapidly cause pain and fatigue. This discomfort must be tolerated in training to develop the muscles so they can better handle the demands of competition sailing.

In addition to the continual muscle strain of hiking in small boat sailing, there is also the need to carry out active movements of the arms and trunk to trim or pump the sail(s), steer and physically drive the boat through waves. The intensity and nature of the physical activity during sailing, and the optimal physical characteristics of the sailors themselves, obviously depend on the class of boat sailed.

▶Research on Hiking

Scientific studies on the demands of small boat sailing have been conducted to examine the toll of sailing on the body. For my scientific study on the physical demands of sailing I selected the Laser class because Laser sailors require excellent hiking endurance to perform well and very little previous research had been done on the subject.

To summarise the procedures, a profile of typical activity in a race (length of legs, frequency of tacking) was developed from analysing video of good Laser class sailors competing in windy (over 12 knots) national level races. A dinghy sailing ergometer was specially designed and constructed for use with the 90-minute race that involved a two-triangle format with upwind legs, tacking and reaching. (A dinghy sailing ergometer is a dry-land device designed to mimic the physical demands of small boat sailing without having to get wet!)

The hiking, sheeting, pumping and trapezing muscles and actions.

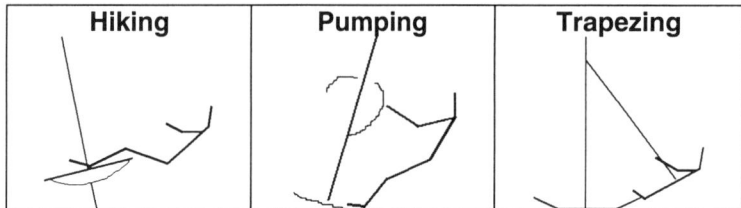

Main muscles	Works hardest*	Action
Knee extensors (Quadricpes)		Hold the legs straight while hiking or standing
Hip flexors (Illiopsoas)		Hold the trunk up while hiking by joining the thighbone, hip and lower back
Foot flexors (Tilialis anterior)		Lift the toes up while hiking
Shoulders (Deltoids)		Pull the arms backwards in sheeting/pumping
Elbow flexors (Biceps)		Bend the arms when sheeting
Hand flexors		Make the hand hold the sheet or boom
Trunk flexors (abdominals)		Stabilise the spine by linking the ribs and pelvis
Back extensors (lower back muscles)		Support the lower back against the range of trunk movements.
Foot extensors (calf muscles)		Point your toes while trapezing or sailboarding.

*While all forms of sailing will use a lot of the body's muscles, the different forms of sailing tax the muscles to varying degrees. Usually a few key muscles fatigue first – and these need special attention in training.

Subjects watched a video of a Laser skipper sailing according to the protocol (on-water), while hiking from the Laser ergometer in a laboratory and performed their normal on-water movements in tandem with the video. This set-up was used to find out exactly what is going on in the body when small boat sailing and what makes one person able to hike harder than another.

►Key Findings

Simulated dinghy sailing raised the subjects' blood pressure sharply and involved a modest and steady rate of energy use by the body. The use of aerobic energy during the three 20 minute upwind legs was 40 to 60 percent of the subjects' maximum – indicating only a moderate level of exertion. However, during the upwind legs, blood pressure was extremely high. In fact, blood pressure levels matched those you'd normally find during really hard bicycle exercise – indicating how strongly the muscles contract when hiking to slow blood flow. As you may expect, both blood pressure and aerobic energy usage were significantly lower during the two 12 minute reaching legs.

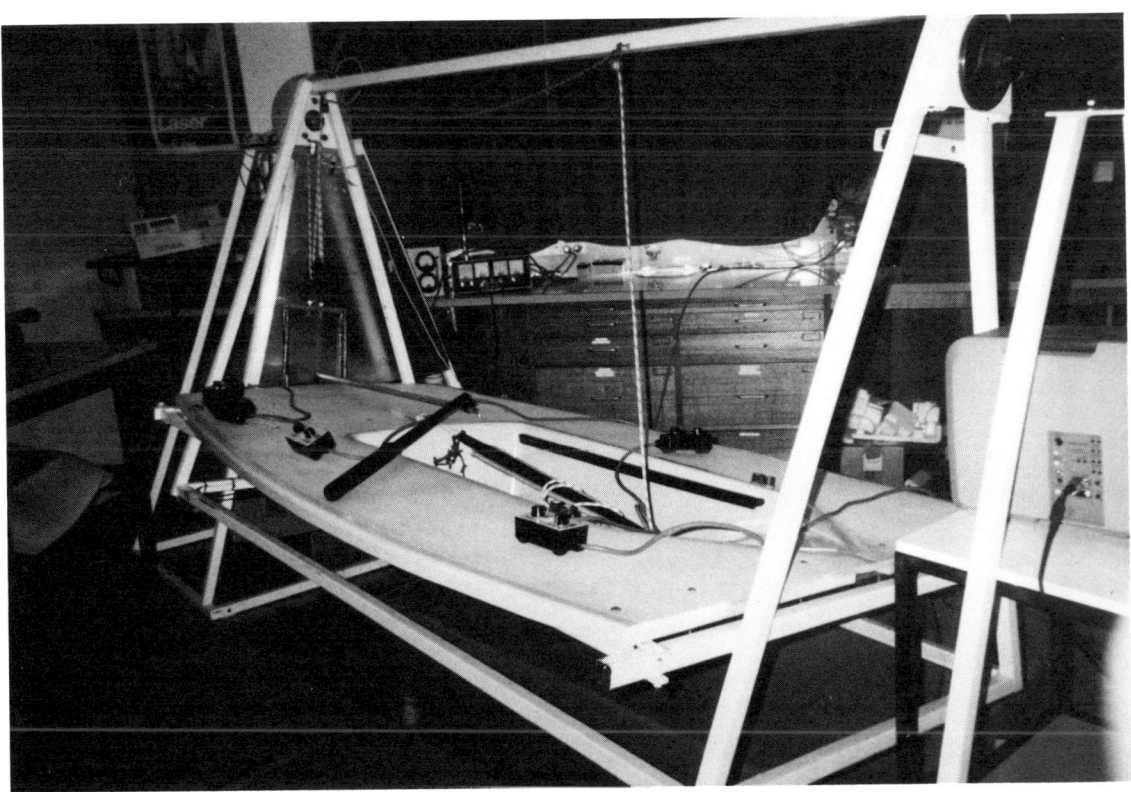

The Laser deck in this sailing simulator heels to leeward to simulate wind. The mainsheet and tiller are weighted with appropriate loads. A computer screen in front of the sailor shows a dynamic course.

Other results indicated that the combination of body mass in sailing clothing, thigh muscle strength, hiking strap length, aerobic fitness and the blood pressure response to hiking all contributed to the sailors' hiking performance. In short, body size, strength and aerobic fitness are all related to how effectively you hike, so it is worth working on these factors.

A separate study determined that around 25 per cent of the thigh muscle's strength is used when hiking. Static contractions of the thigh muscles at this level will fatigue the muscle very quickly – within five minutes. But, the discontinuous nature of hiking – with periodic rest periods thrown in (tacking, going over waves) – allows small boat sailors to sustain the static contractions for much longer than five minutes. In practice, this means that if there is no detrimental effect on the trim of the boat and sail, the body movements you make while hiking can and should be exploited to improve your endurance.

Hiking straps vary in the width of padding, the covering material and the thickness and quality of the padding itself. A covered strap with dense foam padding that will not fold over on itself is probably best so that the instep of the foot is not rubbed raw. Also, make sure the material is not slippery.

Hiking: The thigh muscles do most of the work.

▶What the Results Mean for You

- Hiking performance is related to a number of factors. Most of the righting force that can be produced is determined by the sailor's body mass (including the weight of sailing clothing), his or her standing height, quadriceps muscle strength and endurance and the length the hiking strap is set. The last factor is also related to the endurance of the muscles involved in hiking (quadriceps, hip flexors, abdominal muscles). Setting the hiking strap longer or hiking off the toes allows the body to be held further out and this requires greater muscular effort.

- You can improve your hiking endurance if you momentarily relax or reduce muscle tension every so often to promote blood flow, for example, as you go over a wave. If you can 'tune-in' to the sensations (pain) from the muscles, you will be able to tell when you should relax them. By accurately judging how fatigued the muscles are, you can add rest breaks to stop them becoming too fatigued before the finish. Experience in hiking for long periods and being aware of the effect on your body will help you to pace yourself over a race.

- The further out you can hike – even by hiking with only your toes touching the hiking strap – the faster you will go. The stop-start nature of on-water hiking also explains why leaning from a hiking bench in a completely static position is a great deal harder.

Sail Fitter: Sailing Fitness and Training

Hiking boots are designed to pad the instep of the foot, provide grip, support the ankle and prevent cuts and abrasions. Lace-up boots support the ankle more firmly than the zip or stretchy wet-suit variety. However, a pair of rubber boots on your feet can create some clumsiness when moving around the boat in light winds. Some sailors prefer bare feet to improve their feel.

- Training by leaning from a hiking bench will be more useful when you perform movements that are as similar as possible to actual sailing. Try obtaining a video of yourself or a top competitor sailing and watch it while using a hiking bench, copying the main actions.

- Aerobic training will help to condition the heart and blood vessels to withstand the high blood pressures involved in hiking and may improve hiking endurance at the same time. Cycling is great aerobic exercise for small boat sailors given that the thigh muscles are heavily involved in cycling as in hiking. Rowing on a machine will also be useful for developing the legs while at the same time developing the upper body and arms, so they can better trim the mainsheet. Running is ok, but involves greater impact than cycling or rowing.

- Setting the hiking strap longer (if hiking off the instep of the foot) or hiking off the toes may permit a greater righting moment to be generated by allowing the body to be held further out. Simply, as long as the knees are closer to the gunwale and the trunk is held out as far, the righting moment will be greater. Although leaning out further increases muscle tension and thereby reduces your endurance, it is useful to have a number of hiking positions so you can hike flat-out for powering off the start line and then take it easier on the second beat when you have a good lead! You can also physically train yourself to a point where such a flat-out position can be held for most of the race – then you'll reach the front of the pack!

Good hiking boots and a padded hiking strap can make hiking more comfortable.

Hiking pants with battens on the back of the thigh allow more comfortable hiking. However, they are expensive and can wear by rubbing on non-skid and fittings. To prevent this, try wearing a pair of light-weight lyrca pants over the top of your hiking pants.

- Improving your thigh muscle strength by weight training exercises (e.g., leg extensions, leg presses and squats) should improve your ability to hike from the hiking strap, lessening the common tendency to partly hang off a sheet or stay (or lean on your crew).

- The back of your thighs should be thickly padded to spread the pressure from the relatively sharp edge of the gunwale. This is something anyone can do with little effort. Padding the back of the thighs reduces the physical compression of blood vessels from the gunwale. Stiff battens (approximately 20 cm long down the length of the thigh) sewn into hiking shorts/wetsuits help to smooth out the ride dramatically (but make sure they are comfortable and do not move around). One layer of wetsuit over the back of the thighs is definitely not enough for top performance. Intense pain will certainly interfere with your hiking endurance and boat speed!

▶ Advanced Hiking Technique

I originally thought that the best small boat hiking position involved a bent body, that is, a fair degree of bend at the knee and hip joints with the bottom just skimming the waves. I figured hiking like this would be unbeatable over a long race because the muscles work more efficiently in this position compared with hiking with the legs straight and trunk laid well back. High tension in the muscles when hiking flat-out restricts blood flow and limits the energy available in the muscle, making you tired more quickly. The bent body position is quite difficult to hold properly anyway, so I thought that setting a fitness-training goal of being able to hold this position for a full race would be reasonable. However, I was wrong – there are ways to hike harder.

A couple of top Laser sailors started using a new technique a few years ago and quickly showed great upwind speed. They started hiking as flat out as they could. By tightening their hiking straps they could hike by their toes and in this position were actually forced to keep their legs straight. They had also developed the fitness to lay their bodies nearly flat. The fitness to do this takes years to develop – huge loads are placed on the ankles and the hip muscles since they are not designed to work this way for extended periods. Years are needed to build up the tendons and ligaments of the ankles, knees and hips to withstand the strain.

When weight jackets were banned from sailing in 1997 many expected that Laser sailors' (and other classes) body weight would increase. However, top Laser sailors seem to have remained about the same weight. To compensate, it seems they are hiking further out and more consistently so.

These sailors reasoned that maintaining a high righting moment while sailing the boat flatter would make them faster upwind in a breeze. By tightening the hiking strap and lengthening the tiller they could hike off the tips of their toes with their legs and body extended and held well above the waves and hold both the mainsheet and tiller hands near chest level.

Hiking off the toes and leaning back further is harder but faster.

Basically the aim of the technique is to keep your head almost level with your knees and eyes looking down the end of the tiller extension. It is a funny feeling at first because your head is at a different angle and you can't see as much. And it is physically quite hard. However, you can focus on sailing the boat flatter and on gaining extra speed and height.

To be able to lay your body flatter while hiking it is important to have good flexibility of the hip muscles and to strengthen the abdominal muscles – these muscles are responsible for supporting the trunk while hiking. The more flexible the hip muscles the more relaxed they will be when the trunk is lent back. The stronger the abdominal muscles the better they will support the spine and stop it inverting from the pull of the hip muscles. Therefore, the hip muscles need to be stretched especially well before and after sailing and the abdominals need regular training to help keep the spine in good shape when hiking flat out.

It is interesting to compare how hiking positions have changed with the advent of battens in hiking pants and the 'far-out on-the-toes technique' (see Diagram, next page). The thighs of a sailor wearing only a wetsuit or shorts squash over the gunwale. This restricts blood flow and lowers the body to the oncoming waves. Hiking pants with battens tend to lift your bottom higher off the water and prevent the gunwale stabbing into the back of the thighs.

To lift yourself even higher, tighten the hiking strap so the feet are held down lower and slide thicker battens into the hiking pants. Also, to maximise righting moment, lean back further and hold the hands up high, steering and trimming the sheet from chest level. Of course, the only trouble is the position is much harder to hold! But, it's ideal for blasting off the start line.

A tighter hiking strap actually gives you a good variety of hiking positions. In light to moderate winds where you don't need to hike so hard you can sit in slightly and hike off the instep of your feet. Since you're locked in tightly to the hull in this position it makes it easier to 'torque' the boat – that is, steer it by throwing your body forward or back. On the reaches the tighter strap makes it easier to keep your posterior out of the waves. Then when it really blows, simply slide out to your toes – there's no need to adjust the length of the strap and you have a variety of hiking positions.

Repeating the earlier warning: hiking off the toes must be approached gradually to strengthen the ankles. The best way to do this may be to tighten the strap gradually over a period of months and slowly spend more time swinging from your toes.

Note that your height and the design of the boat will determine whether hiking off the toes or the instep of the feet is best. If you are taller than 180cm or so you probably will be able to get out far enough by hiking off the instep. Shorter, like me, and hiking from lower down the foot seems to feel more powerful with a tighter strap.

Note that on some dinghies, the hiking strap is so close to the gunwale that your knees are naturally within a few centimetres of the gunwale. In this case, you will have little choice but to hike off the instep of your feet.

Harder hiking: with the advent of battened hiking pants and more aggressive hiking, the top sailors hike with their bodies further out and bottoms riding higher above the waves to sail faster and point higher.

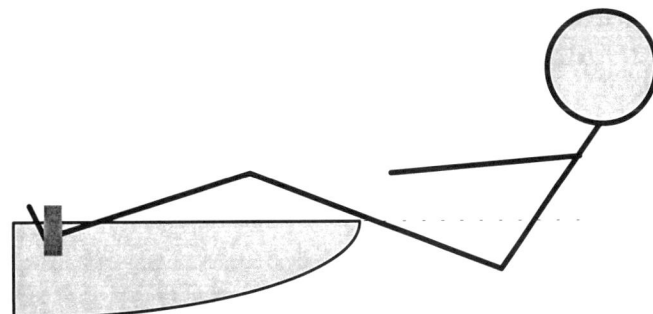

Wet-suit only.

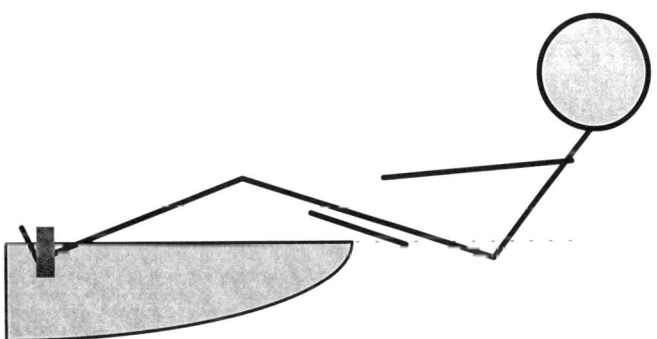

Hiking pants with battens.

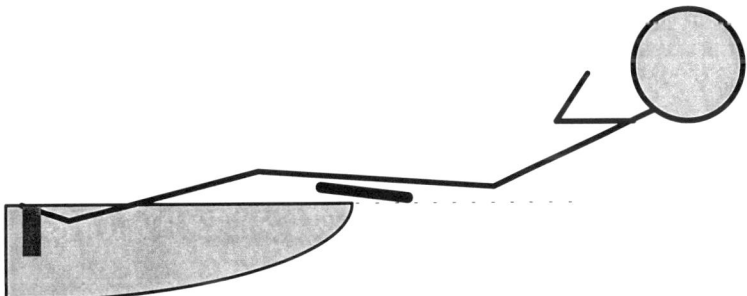

Hiking pants, thicker battens, hiking off toes, tight strap, arms high, leaning further back.

▶▶4. TRAPEZING FITNESS

To get a small boat going really fast upwind, you need to hang in a trapeze. This is great, just hang there and trim the sails and take off! No more hiking!

However, usually a trapeze means a bigger boat with bigger sails, so the emphasis in training shifts up the body to the trunk, shoulders and arms that control the sails and thereby your boat's speed. Also, you have to get on and off the trapeze efficiently, so there is also a need for good balance and agility.

A simple look at what a trapezing crew does suggests what sort of supplementary training they should do. There are long periods where the body stays relatively still on trapeze. As with hiking, many muscles are working statically to help hold the position - abdominal, calf and neck muscles.

Then, there are bursts of more active work – tacking, gybing, hoisting and lowering a spinnaker. A couple of these activities done in a row will elevate your heart rate dramatically. Therefore, you can do more interval training (eg, circuit training in a gym) than hiking sailors, because there are distinct work and rest periods.

As with hiking, the muscles that contract statically during trapezing will benefit from being relaxed occasionally to allow the blood to flow fully. So, by all means make small movements of the legs and arms to enhance blood flow. These movements can also aid the speed of the boat, as you'll see below.

▶The Harness

There are two basic styles of harness – the nappy and the more adjustable strap-around varieties. The former is more common in skiff classes and the latter in other dinghies. This is probably because the skiff sailor often trapezes more upright, squeezing the groin more firmly. Women trapezing flatter on, say, a 470, can get a better fit from a more adjustable harness.

To improve comfort and lower back support, harnesses often have a moveable pad or battens running vertically down the back of the harness.

When sizing up a new harness, look for:
- A snug fit around the hips.
- A spreader bar. The all-important hook is attached to the harness either by a small plate and ropes or a wider spreader bar and, often, adjustable straps. The spreader bar ensures the harness provides more comfortable hip support and less pinching.
- Adjustable straps, including on either side of the hook and around the legs.

- A shoulder strap that is long enough to strap over a life jacket and other clothes.
- Material over the shoulders that is finished off as smoothly as possible to avoid skin irritation.
- Battens sewn into the back of the harness for support.

The position of the hook and that steel bar which spreads the weight across the hips is quite important. It needs to sit relatively low on the body (slightly below the belly button) to provide effective leverage and to support the pelvis. Additionally, a bigger gap between the tip of the hook and the harness allows more room for error when hooking up.

▶ Donning the Nappy

The trapeze harness usually goes on the outside of all clothing. Step in and pull the harness up. Throw the shoulder strap over and fasten tight so that the shoulders have to be slightly hunched. This ensures a good fit, as the harness will ride up when you're first on the wire. The trapeze harness should be sufficiently tight between the groin and shoulders so that the trunk and shoulders are supported when flat-out. If the harness is not tight enough you may find that the abdominal muscles are a little more tired at the end of the day and your shoulders are sore.

The straps attached to the spreader bar should be firm so that once on the trapeze the distance between your tummy and the hook is minimal – not more than 10 cm. With the hook in a consistent position in relation to your body you will develop a feel for its position and hook and unhook without looking.

Tuck in all the harness straps so they don't catch on the rigging. However, you may like to leave the shoulder strap adjustable so you can loosen the load if the wind goes light and you're stuck inboard. Anyway, more often than not you will need to re-adjust the harness soon after you first hit the wire for a better fit, usually by tightening the shoulder strap.

▶ Trapezing Technique

When you're still getting used to trapezing you struggle to find a balance between stability (feet wide apart) and maximum righting moment (feet together, toes pointed, body flat). With experience in the boat's movement and practice you will gain confidence in your position and get your feet closer together.

It is important to be able to adjust the height at which you trapeze. As a rough guide, the lowest you want the boat's trapeze rings is at the level of the gunwales when measured next to the gunwales. At its highest, you will be trapezing with your feet flat on the deck, legs bent at 90 degrees – as though you are sitting in a chair.

In light winds you won't hit the wire, but avoid taking the harness off – you never know! Loosen the shoulder straps and try not to get the hook caught on anything!

In moderate winds trapeze higher. This way you can swing out from crouching on the deck to fully extended with ease, but not generate so much righting moment that you will pull the boat too far over.

Once it's fresh enough that you can trapeze all the time, go much lower on the wire. It is important to keep the shoulders back and the legs straight. Get used to looking around at the water, other boats, etc. from this strange angle. For maximum leverage, point the toes and keep a spare arm above your head, if you don't have too much on!

You need to keep your weight out there consistently. You can't get out any further, so you really just have to hang there and provide a stable righting moment.

You also have a good vantage point from your position and so should feed information back to the skipper on wind, waves and competitors.

The fit of the harness over the shoulders and around the hips is vital for comfortable trapezing.

▶ Tacking

When you hear the call of 'ready about', 'ok' 'lets go' or 'ya right?' you can either unhook while still out there or move in a little, then unhook. You may like to brush your other hand down to make sure the hook is cleared. As the boat flattens and turns through the wind, bend your knees to move in and through the boat.

Try to get out on the new tack as quickly as possible, hanging from the handle, and then hooking on when ready.

Of course, this technique varies on different boats. For example, 49er sailors don't unhook until they're half way in because they will stand upright during the tack – the ring usually falls off. Some sailors have become used to propping on the side deck and hooking up, others prefer to go straight out and then hook up. Nonetheless, it's vital to get fully out as soon as possible, so practice hanging from the hook with one arm and then hooking up without looking.

▶ Advanced techniques

In marginal trapezing conditions you may like to trapeze with your feet on the centreboard case or mast so you're on the wire earlier, ready to slide out with an increase in wind. It also means you can react more subtly to the wind and effectively trim the boat via small movements forward, back in and out.

On a fresh beat, work hard at making sure your shoulders are back at the tops of waves to help keep the boat flat and accelerate down the back of waves. You need to be quite low on the trapeze in these conditions to maximize your leverage. This makes it a little more difficult to get inboard for a tack, so you could adjust yourself up a little just before the tack. Don't lower yourself so far that you're skimming more than 1 in 20 or so waves with your back. Raise yourself for the reaches and when less righting moment is needed.

The trapeze allows the crew to quickly move forward and backward along the gunwale, especially when sailing downwind. You should take advantage of this to adjust the fore and aft trim of the hull – move forward to keep the stern from dragging and shuffle back to lift the bow and crack the boat onto the plane. It's also a good idea to move backwards when rounding the top mark and on tight reaches to reduce the chance of the rudder cavitating and the bow digging in.

Small movements on trapeze are especially beneficial when sailing in waves. You can do some little pushes backward through your feet to help nudge the boat down waves on reaches and runs. These pushes combined with moving in or out on the trapeze can do much to help the skipper trim and steer the boat, reducing his or her need to work hard with the rudder. However, the timing of these movements is critical and much practice is needed to coordinate them effectively with the wind, waves and your skipper.

In big winds and waves your body and/or feet can be slammed by a big wave and you risk getting washed off the gunwale. Falling sideways into the gunwale or skipper is slow! There are a few ways to save you this embarrassment:
- Try trapezing slightly higher.
- Let the skipper know what's coming in the next 5-15 meters so that he or she can heel the boat briefly to get you higher above the waves.

- Lock one foot flat against the gunwale for a better grip. Or, lift one leg off briefly to avoid the wave.
- Use the sheet to brace yourself.
- Grab the trapeze rope and pull it sharply towards your head to pull yourself up for a moment.
- Do a quick 'bum lift' to avoid a wave heading straight for your behind.

Once you have achieved the basics of efficiently moving around the boat and getting on and off the trapeze you can start to experiment with the more advanced trapezing techniques. In the future crews will probably make improvements in their trapezing technique by mastering small movements around the boat that increase boat speed. They will also use their prime position out the side of the boat to feed quality information back to the skipper.

▶▶5. SAILBOARDING FITNESS

Sailboarding became a real athletes' sport when the International Sailing Federation changed the rules to allow unlimited pumping of the sail. It has been likened to doing pull-ups for 45 minutes on a constantly moving balance beam.

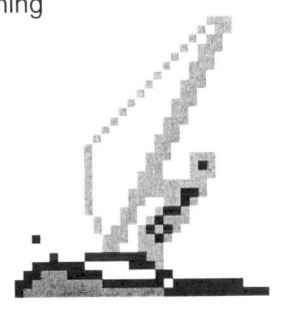

When accelerating off the start line top sailboarders will pump the sail at a rate up to 120 pumps per minute. Obviously, this intensity cannot be sustained and once in clear air they slow down a little. However, the tactical challenge of sailing remains – with a different twist – if you go the wrong way you have to pump twice as hard to get back!

Since it's physically more intense, typical sailboard races are set to last only 30-45 minutes. As with dinghy sailing, you should aim to develop a fair amount of your fitness from spending time on the water.

Balance and muscular endurance will help you get around the corners quickly on a sailboard.

Weakening of the handgrip from 'blowing up' of the forearms is the most obvious area of fatigue when sailboarding. The forearm muscles are relatively small but much is required of them. As a result, blood is shunted to the area, lactic acid builds up and the muscles' strength falls. These static contractions of the forearm muscles (and many others) are a feature of sailboarding. As with hiking, phasing these contractions on and off will dramatically increase your endurance. So, try to release or change your grip on the boom every so often and make full use of your harness to lighten the load on your forearms.

On the land, your training should reflect the shorter, more intense nature of the discipline with more intense, briefer exercise sessions than a hiking sailor. A suitable training session for a sailboarder could consist of: a five-minute warm-up, a 2000m time trial on a rowing machine, 50 crunches, 50 body pull-ups (see Appendix), a second 2000m timed row, finished off with a warm-down and a stretch. This workout (lasting about 30 min) targets aerobic fitness and muscle endurance in fairly specific exercises to sailboarding.

Cross-training in a sport like indoor rock climbing can also be good for developing the larger back muscles, grip strength, balance and agility needed by board sailors.

Sailboarders effectively balance between four points – two feet and two hands, but mostly by the feet. This leaves a lot of the body in between. Like an unstayed mast, the body will not be supported properly unless there are strong 'side stays'. Therefore, particular attention should be paid to the lower back and abdominal muscles that stabilise the trunk. Once these areas are strong, your ability to transfer power from the legs and trunk through to the arms and to the sail will increase.

The shoulders and upper back can also be a source of discomfort for the sailboarder. This is because you're always pulling at the boom with extended arms and shoulders and this is not a natural position. An exercise like scapular retraction (under Seated row in the Appendix) can strengthen the muscles in the upper back and keep your shoulders in a good functional position.

Sailboarders are allowed to carry a 'camelback' which is a soft container, filled with up to 1 litre of fluid. Indeed, you should take a drink to replenish lost body fluid during the course of a race.

▶▶6. HOW TO SPEND YOUR SAILING TIME

One training day, I left shore with Australian Gold medallist Tom King working on his 470, parts and tools spread out around the boat park. When I returned about four hours later he was still at it. I had seen similar scenes day after day and asked him why he didn't get more on water time. He reckoned that there was a 470 class rule that you needed to do three hours of boat work for every one-hour on the water. He was getting ready to sail overseas so he had to get his boat work hours up!

In practice, Tom got ample on-water time in a very well prepared boat and despite my relative lack of Laser boat work I rarely had any breakdowns on the water. It showed me how important allocating the right amount of time to the many aspects of your preparation can be – fitness, boat maintenance, weather, psychology and rules.

In the strictest one-design single-handed classes such as Laser, 49er and Mistral, physical training on-shore or on-water will make up a sizeable portion of total training time because less boat work is needed. The Europe class is also single-handed and requires excellent hiking fitness to sail fast, but the class rules allow for greater differences in mast, sail and gear combinations, so proportionally more time should go to obtaining and testing equipment. At the far end of the spectrum, America's Cup teams spend an enormous amount of time designing and tuning boats and rigs.

So, I came up some percentages to illustrate where the priorities might lie for each class (see chart). Of course, this is only my rough guide as to how much of your available time you should spend in each area. You should also consider your strengths and weaknesses. For example, if you are unfit, but can trim a boat well and pick shifts easily, you can allocate more time to physical training.

Note that there is a significant cross-over in the five items in the chart which increase the importance of sailing fitness – Fitness can contribute to the boat's speed through, say, hiking endurance. Also, fitness will influence boat handling, say, a spinnaker hoist or recovery from a capsize.

You can also see by the chart that I suggest that a 49er crew should spend about 30% of the time they devote to sailing on improving their boat's speed. Rig settings, sail and hull trim and fitness all influence boat speed, so they contribute to this 30% as well. This time allocation is slightly less than a 470 crew because the 49er is more of a true one-design class while the 470 allows a number of sailmakers in the class. Yngling crews may like to spend more time on psychology, considering there are three in the team and that requires greater on-board coordination.

Nowadays, top dinghy sailors know they must prepare themselves, their boat and their skills impeccably. The question is, in what proportion?

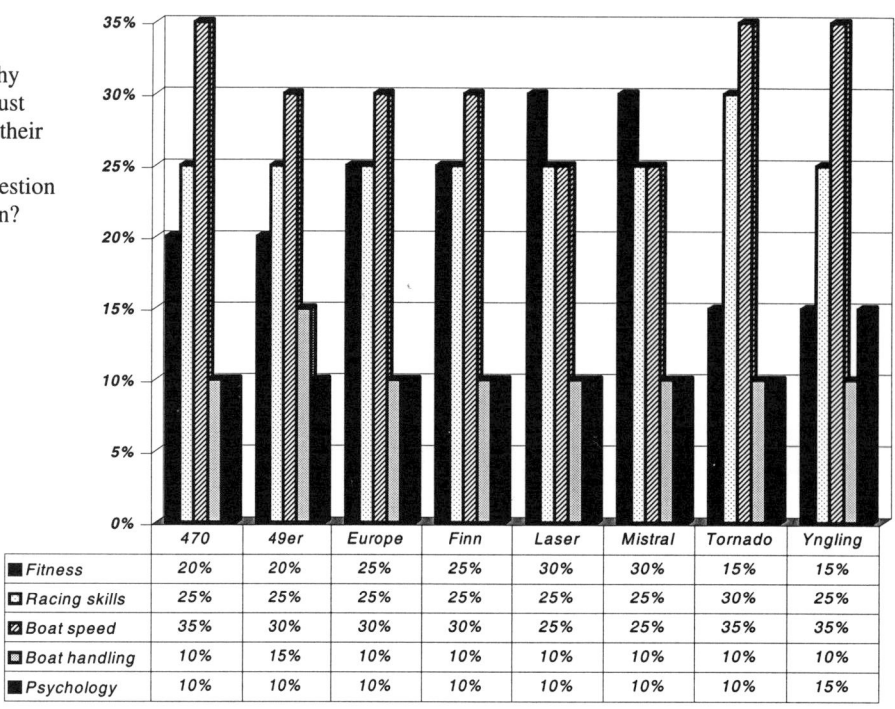

	470	49er	Europe	Finn	Laser	Mistral	Tornado	Yngling
■ Fitness	20%	20%	25%	25%	30%	30%	15%	15%
☐ Racing skills	25%	25%	25%	25%	25%	25%	30%	25%
▨ Boat speed	35%	30%	30%	30%	25%	25%	35%	35%
☐ Boat handling	10%	15%	10%	10%	10%	10%	10%	10%
■ Psychology	10%	10%	10%	10%	10%	10%	10%	15%

Suggested percentage time to be spent on each facet of sailboat racing by class. Note: Racing skills = starting, strategy and tactics.

You may care to develop a chart like that above of your own, for the class of boat you sail. Start by carefully evaluating your strengths and weaknesses and then allocate your time accordingly.

▶▶7. TOP SEVEN TRAINING SESSIONS

Below are some of my favourite high-quality training sessions that improve sailing performance. Use these as a guide to the types of activities that can be done on a daily basis. Having a repertoire of sessions that you are happy to do ensures quality and variety in your training and encourages you to stick to your training program.

▶No.7 – Postural/hiking muscles: Crunch and reverse sit-ups

Important for posture and to prevent low back problems, these core abdominal exercises are also beneficial for hiking, trapezing and sailboarding. 'Crunches' use the abdominal muscles to raise the shoulders and upper back off the ground while leaving the lower back planted, legs bent. Reverse sit-ups involve lying down flat and raising the feet up over your head (bent or straight-legged) to work the hips and abdominals (see the Appendix (abdominal exercises) for complete descriptions).

In terms of crunches and reverse sit-ups, a good workout may involve sets (repetitions of 10 to 20) completed in the natural breaks you find in other training sessions. For example, try four or five sets of 20 interspersed with a weight training routine. This is no speed test however; slowly raise and then hold the shoulders, or legs up for two seconds to emphasise the static nature of the hiking effort in your training. Also, following every training session, stretch the hip and lower back muscles to improve these muscles' suppleness, reduce stiffness and minimise the potential for lower back soreness while sailing.

Once you are up to easily completing, say, 30 repetitions of crunches/reverse sit-ups, you can try one or two of the more advanced abdominal exercises in the Appendix. These exercises put higher loads on the abdominal and hip muscles and can be introduced after these muscles have been strengthened over a period of weeks using simpler exercises. There are more examples the Appendix. As you can see there are heaps of variations. There is no need to do them all at once. Instead use, say, two variations per training session.

Crunch: A partial sit-up in which you lift the trunk, but not the lower back, off the floor. Therefore, the hip flexor muscles are not involved.

Reverse sit-up: Lay flat on ground, knees slightly bent. Lift both feet up, and well over your head and lower to just above the ground.

▶ No.6 – Hiking and sheeting endurance: Wall-sit and body pull up

These are very simple and practical exercise that are relevant to hiking and sheeting and can be done without equipment, for example, when away from home.

For the wall sit, stand with your back against a solid wall then slide down (moving the feet out in front) until the legs are bent at around $90°$ to $130°$. If this is too easy then holding a weight or bending the knees more can increase the resistance. Sailboarders could place a wobble board under their feet to also train their stability.

For the body pull-up, lie face-up on the floor under the edge of a table and wrap you fingers around the edge of the table. Your arms should be near straight and hands about shoulder-width apart. With knees bent about 90 degrees, pull your chest up to touch the underside of the table and lower.

A minimum of 10 to 30 minutes wall-sitting (interrupted by body pull-ups) will make this session worthwhile. For example, work on a four-minute rotation: Start with two minutes of wall-sitting, then hop under the table and do 20 body pulls at your leisure, aiming to finish just before the four minutes is up. Repeat the rotation five times, increasing the duration of the wall-sit slightly each time, to total 20 minutes.

▶ No.5 – Muscle Strength: Weight training

Upper body strength is vital in small boat sailing so you can effectively manipulate the rope controls – and lift your boat! Below is a list of key exercises that focus on the arms, shoulders, back and chest and are thus relevant for sailors:

You'll find complete descriptions of all gym exercises mentioned here in the Appendix.

Shoulders	• Lateral raises • Bent-over lateral raise • Upright row
Upper Back/Biceps	• Bicep curl • Chin-ups • Hammer curls • Seated rowing (one or two-arm) • 1-arm dumbbell row
Chest	• Push-ups • Bench press

A general principle of weight training is to do fewer repetitions per set (eg, four sets of 4 to 10 reps) to build strength and more repetitions per set to develop muscular endurance (eg, two sets of 15 to 40 reps). For sailors in pre-season training it may be best to do, say, four to eight weeks of strength training followed by six weeks of muscular endurance work. This acts to build muscle strength then uses that strength to enhance the muscles' endurance and get them in the best shape for working the sails.

Also, progressively increase the weight you lift over a period of weeks. Improvements in strength and muscle endurance from weight training can only be expected with a minimum of two to three sessions a week, so pay up your gym fees and get it to it properly. Otherwise, concentrate on other activities mentioned here.

Sample upper-body weight training session to build strength for sailing. Such a session would follow two to four weeks of lifting lighter weights to build up the joints, tendons and ligaments. Begin with 10 minutes warm-up and stretching.

Body part	Exercise	Repetitions	Rest between sets	Sets
Back & biceps	Chin-up	4-7	90 sec	3
	Seated row	6-8	90 sec	4
Chest	Bench press	6-8	90 sec	4
Shoulders	Upright row	8	90 sec	3
	Bent-over lateral raise	6-8	90 sec	3
Lower back	Back extension	20	(start next exercise)	3
Abdominals	Crunches	30	60 sec; then start next set of Back ext.	3

Sample upper-body weight training session to build muscular endurance for sailing. This type of session would normally follow four to eight weeks of strength training. Begin with a good warm-up and stretching.

Exercise #1	Repetitions	Exercise #2	Repetitions	Rest between sets	Sets
1-arm seated row	25 (each arm)	Bench press	15	60 sec; then start next set of seated row	3
Upright row	20	Forearm plank	2 min (15 sec on; 5 sec off)	90 sec; then start next set of upright row	3
1-arm dumbbell row	15 (each arm)	Bicep curl	20	60 sec; then start next of dumbbell row	2
Back extension	25	Crunches	40	60 sec; then start next set of back extensions	2

If you do three strength-training sessions a week, let one of those be a hard session, where the weights you lift are about your highest level. For the other two sessions, reduce the load by about 10% for one and 20% for the other. Do the hardest session when you are freshest. Adjusting the loading like this reduces the risk of injury and overtraining, yet it still provides a good enough stimulus to improve your muscles' strength.

Strength and muscular endurance training can also be done for the leg muscles. In particular, the quadriceps can be developed using exercises such as leg presses, squats and leg extensions (see Appendix). These can be added to the above sample sessions to improve thigh strength and hiking endurance. However, it may be better to do most of your heavy leg workouts either on the water, on a hiking bench or on a bike. This ensures that the legs are trained specifically for the job they do on the water.

▶ No.4 – Endurance: Exercise bike and rowing machine

First, do three minutes of light pedalling on an exercise bike, increasing effort to achieve a heart rate of 130 to 160 beats a minute (moderate to heavy breathing) over the next 17 minutes. A heart rate monitor can be used to determine your heart rate or you can simply take your own pulse at your wrist. Get off the bike and stretch the legs.

"Sheeting" on a rowing machine is a great simulation of the on-water action.

Next, with the legs straight, sitting on a rowing machine, begin pulling the rowing handle with each arm, alternately. Pull lightly at first to get the blood to the arms. Then do six pulls at about 85 per cent plus effort, trying to simulate the sheeting action on your boat as well as you can, then swap arms and do another six pulls. Continue for six minutes to approximate the duration of a reach.

Back to the bike. Repeat the above 20 minute cycling effort before doing another solid set of arm pulls on the rowing machine and a final lighter and shorter effort on the bike to finish off. This makes for a good hour-long high aerobic session, concentrating on lower body endurance and upper body power movements, just like sailing.

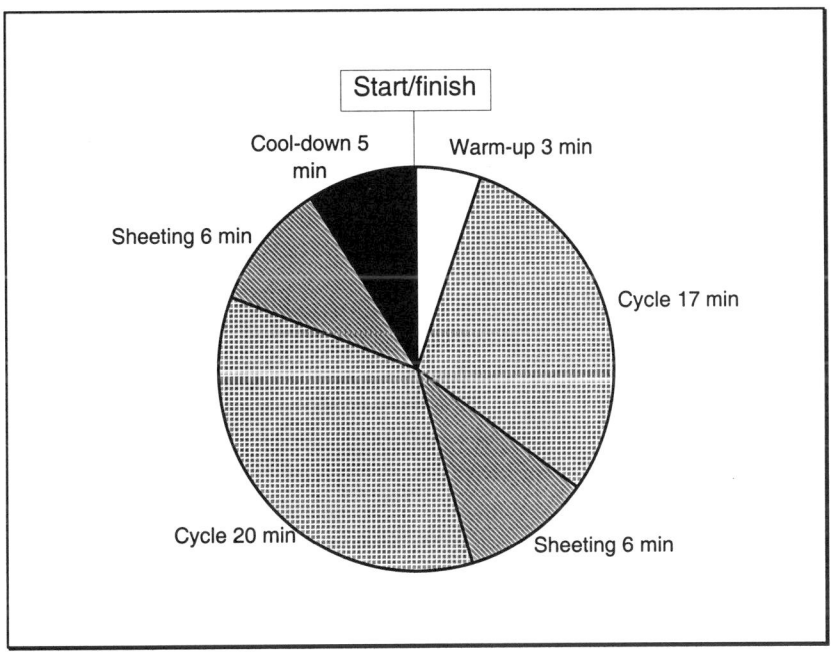

▶ No.3 – Endurance: Cycling

A favourite of many top small boat sailors, sustained cycling promotes the development of the aerobic system and thigh muscles and the circulation. Also, at high intensities it can be a good physical challenge of similar duration to sailing races.

Generally, youths will find it quite easy to fit in a ride of 10 to 20 minutes or more five times a week to school and home at a light to moderate pace and this is a good basic level of cycling training for most people. For off-season work on a bike I like to vary my training between one of three basic types of sessions: (1) long-slow endurance: a continuous effort of longer than 90 minutes at a moderate intensity; (2) moderate aerobic: 45 to 75 minutes of continuous, moderate to high intensity cycling, and; (3) heavy aerobic: extended periods of heavy work with rest breaks – mainly done up and down hills and over longer straight stretches for about 45 minutes.

Having a good bike that is comfortable to ride and suits your body size is a priority in cycle training as it motivates you to get on it in the first place.

▶ No.2 – The Simulator: Hiking bench and land boat training

No wind, too much wind, too cold, broken mast and so on are all good excuses not to do your scheduled on-water session. In these situations you can bring your sailing simulator out to play. There are a few different ways to go about this, depending on what you sail.

Go for a short run, ride or skip to get the circulation going, and then stretch all your tight muscles before beginning your simulator exercises.

For hikers, plan to stay hiking (on and off) for 10 to 30 minutes or more to get some benefit, and longer to approximate the duration of a long-course race.

There are a number of variations that can be used to help focus. You could watch a video of yourself sailing, trying to mimic the actions and thoughts that would take place on the water while hiking. You could attach a 'mainsheet' (made of rope and shock cord) and hold a tiller extension in the other hand to simulate your sheeting and steering actions. Or, just watch TV, read a book or listen to music while hiking. Whatever, include 'tacks' in your routine to give yourself a break and to (albeit temporarily) increase the comfort level.

It's not hard to make yourself a hiking bench out of wood or fibreglass and appropriate designs can be found, for example, on Laser class websites. First, measure the dimensions of your boat, particularly the distance from the hiking strap to the gunwale. Use heavy screws or bolts to secure the pieces together because you'll be placing quite a load on the bench, as you get fitter.

Once completed, you should add a 'hike-o-matic' – a round bar placed under and perpendicular to the longitudinal frame of the bench. The bench is now a mini sea-saw, which will rock back when you hike hard enough. You can put markings on the bench and move the bar in or out to adjust how hard you need to hike to rock backwards. Now, you can actually record how long and how hard you are hiking.

It's difficult to set-up a simulator for a crew of a two-handed boat, so it's easier to anchor your boat solidly on its trolley or trailer, jump in and do boat-handling work. The boat should be rigged with all relevant ropes and make sure the boom is at the right height. Sheets can be tied off or shock cord added to simulate the wind. Practice moving through the boat during a tack and pay attention to where each hand and foot fall. Try to develop a consistent pattern of movement. Practice spinnaker sets and gybes in a similar fashion.

Training in the boat but on land is useful to develop technique in a controlled environment.

▶ No.1 – Sailing

From forty-five minutes to four hours sailing in winds greater than 10 knots is great for developing your sailing fitness. Any less and you've wasted your time rigging! Much more and the quality of training may drop to the extent that fatigue interferes with the learning of new skills.

Here are some examples of on-water activities that also give the body a good workout:

On-water fitness work for strong-winds.

- Working on boat speed and sail trim at a high intensity for short periods.
- Repeated laps around a very short course.
- Close reaching.
- Long upwind hiking stints.
- Applying a very close cover to another boat upwind.
- Wearing heavier clothing on the trunk to increase the work done by the hip and abdominal muscles.

If you're after a good workout on the water but the wind is a little lighter than necessary, try the following:

On-water fitness work for lighter winds.

- Turn all your ratchet blocks off.
- Do not wear hiking pants or a harness for sailboarders.
- Tack every 15 metres in a race against a training partner.
- Stage races where pumping and rocking are allowed.

There is no substitute for time on the water.

If the wind turns even lighter and you still want a sailing workout, it's time to quickly paddle back to shore and start work on your simulator.

On-water sailing is plainly best for fitness development because the gains in fitness are exactly in the right areas. Therefore, the training will be of higher quality and more efficient despite the extra time spent rigging, unrigging, getting changed and so on. Other advantages over land-based training include discovering things that do not happen very often – especially in terms of the weather, waves and boat handling – and sailing is often more fun. See the chapter 'On-Water Training' for more sailing training drills.

Warming-up for getting wet: it is important to get the blood flowing well and the muscles warm and stretched before working yourself hard in on-water training. After rigging and getting changed do some stretches before lifting the boat and getting on the water. Once on the water, do lighter activity for the first 10 to 15 minutes, such as semi-hiking and playing the sheet. Then, have another good stretch of the main muscle groups (holding for 10 seconds: hamstring, hip, thigh, arms, shoulders and lower back) for five minutes before the serious hard work. I also find it useful to relax the main muscle groups with stretching again in the middle of a hard session, or between races.

Cool-down: just as important as warming-up is helping the muscles and body to recover after a session. The sail into shore usually provides a form of lighter activity that marks the start of your cool-down. Since the boat needs to be packed away and you need to get changed into some dry clothes, usually the most convenient thing to do next is stretch in the shower. The warm-water helps the muscles to relax, allowing you to give them a really good stretch. I like to finish the cool-down with a further 10 – 20 minutes of more serious stretching at home to reduce muscle soreness and improve flexibility.

In the first edition of this book I wrote, "It's extremely rare to see any small boat sailor stretch, bend or otherwise limber up before the start of a race." However, in the last few years on the water I have seen more bottoms pointing skyward and awkward posing on little boats than ever before. All in the cause of getting a good stretch!

It's not hard to get the muscles into a better working condition, particularly following a heavy race the day before. When showering after a heavy race, stretches can be done of all the stiff muscles to help dissipate some soreness straight away. Later that day, any specific muscles that remain stiff can be relieved by stretching and self-massage. Finally, when getting ready for the next day's race the muscles can again be warmed-up by some aerobic exercise and by stretching the heavily used muscles – legs, arms, back and shoulders mostly.

Lower back stretch: place one foot beside the knee of the opposite leg. With the opposite arm against the bent knee, twist the trunk around.

Quadriceps and hip flexor stretch: start in a kneeling position then reach back with your hand to grab the opposite foot, gently pulling the foot to your bottom. Keep the trunk upright and abdominals tight.

Hamstring stretch: extend one leg straight in front (other leg bent). Slowly reach forward, grasping the ankle or toes for extra leverage.

Chest and biceps stretch: clasp the hands behind the lower back then slowly extend them backwards and upwards.

Bottom stretch: with one leg crossed in front of you, bend forward at the waist. Take a grip on the gunwale for leverage.

▶ Top 7 Session Summary

All intensities and durations of the above sessions can be individualised to your fitness level. The sessions are designed for those who have already completed some background training (especially aerobic exercise). Therefore, untrained sailors should begin with lighter workloads to allow a build-up period. The main point is to give your mind every chance during races by training your body to increase stamina, strength and suppleness so that any suffering and soreness are not a constant distraction.

You do need to push yourself to really improve.

Occasionally, remember to search inside yourself and ask what would happen if I pushed myself a little harder? – Would it help me achieve my goals? Also, consider also things like 'what would happen if I leant back a little bit further when hiking?' Would the boat go faster?

A good training partner is invaluable in this regard. Over a number of years I've been lucky enough to have good training partners who have made me work harder in training. For example, training one week with Laser Gold Medallist Ben Ainslie, we went on a long run together. We started at a moderate pace, chatting and looking over the countryside. Then we turned for home. I increased the pace a little; he responded and increased it a little more. I strode up to match him again. We were a few kilometres from home and I knew I didn't have a good sprint, so I went hard and put a gap between us. I was near maximum effort coming up the last hill but he was still right on my tail so I pushed hard again through to the finish.

It was a meaningless little run, but each of us benefited by exercising harder than we would alone, through competition.

Conversely... this approach must be balanced: Don't overtrain. Don't injure yourself. For example, I know that when I go to the gym for an early morning strength session it cannot be my best because my body is not ready for maximum strength work. I know because I have tried and injured myself by straining too hard. So, to really improve – extend your comfort zone with safe exercising and good technique.

▶▶8. YEARLY TRAINING

Another season rolls around and you start to prepare for the on-water fury. You've read up a bit on training, sailing and winning and know what sort of training exercises to do to sail fitter. But have you got a plan? You know what physical training to do, but when should you do it? You need to work out a yearly plan, that is, to *periodise* your training sessions into a master formula that will produce a peak in fitness when you need it most.

Periodisation has been adopted by coaches of all top-flight sports as a professional way of monitoring and scheduling the effort spent in training so that it leads to the athletes' best performance in the long-term. It involves dividing the year into a number of basic periods that are characterised by the sort of training done and the importance of upcoming competitions. Since the competitions are the important part of the plan, the first step is to chart their dates and then build the training plan back from there.

The overriding goal is to arrive at the main competition in the best possible physical shape. This requires regular training that tapers off just before the main event. The reason for tapering before a regatta is to give the body time to recover, rest and gather strength before undertaking the real challenge of a regatta. It is the taper that actually allows you to reach peak fitness.

Regular training is designed to provide an ongoing barrage of stresses that we can recover from and adapt to. However, many of the specific exercises and workouts we do actually take several days to have their total positive effect (we call this the cumulative effect of training). For example, about eight days pass before the effects of aerobic training are noticed. As a result, since serious sailors might only take one day off or have one easy day per week, it is rare that they are fully recovered during training. This is acceptable during training because no one is keeping score. And, after all, the goal during training is to achieve the fastest possible accumulation of these positive stresses and rests that we can safely handle. The end result, however, is that we are almost never completely rested and recovered during prolonged training and therefore not really at peak fitness.

The yearly training chart on the next page illustrates a basic structure and progression of a yearly training plan with all its ups and downs and different periods. Let's have a look at the principles of each period.

▶ Background Training

Background training involves a gradual increase in your training load (the amount of practice and physical conditioning). This occurs over an extended period which sees the body being built-up steadily – joints become stronger, flexibility increases, muscle coordination is developed, and so on. You can include a variety of activities – sailing, weight training, running, swimming, cycling, aerobics, wall-sitting,

When your target event is many months away, it can be difficult to maintain the motivation to do the background training needed to build yourself to a real peak. You wonder 'is it really worth the effort when there are no guarantees of the outcome?'

trapeze work, plus stretching for flexibility – which will give you a good base in aerobic and muscular conditioning.

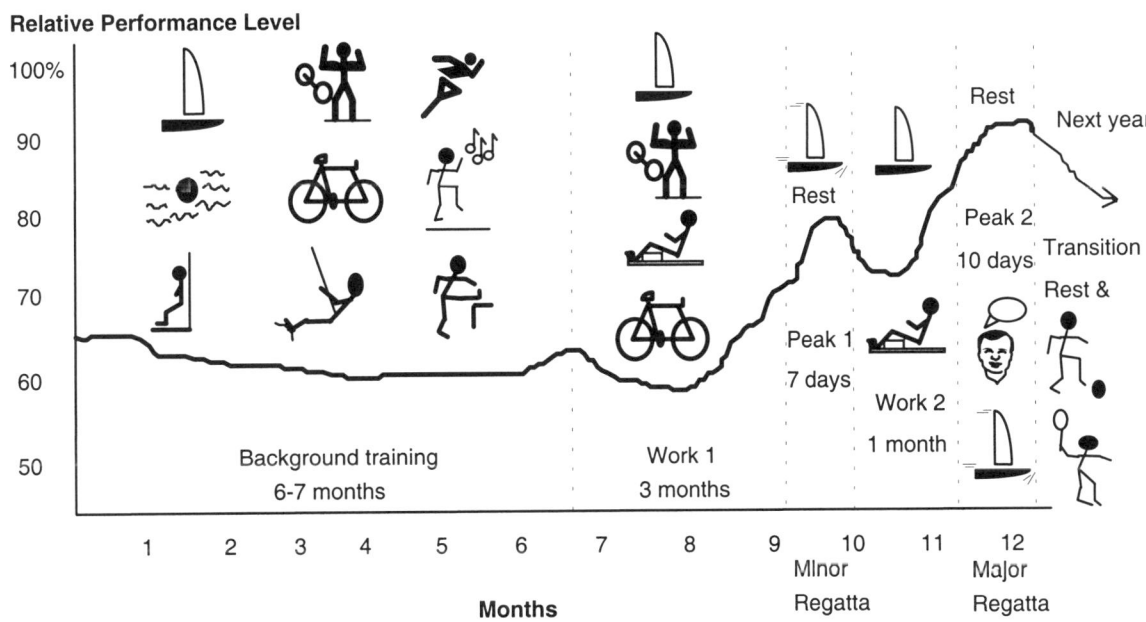

A key is short-term goal setting: the achievement of many small goals act as steps to the far-off objective. Set a specific, measurable and realistic goal for all parts of your training. For instance, aim to lower your time on a 20 km cycling time trial by two minutes in eight weeks; aim to do 15 minutes of stretching after every sailing session and so on. Your attitude will improve along with your fitness.

Most of the background training is high in volume (many hours) but low in intensity (medium effort) because this encourages the fundamental development of all physical capacities. Although technical, tactical and psychological preparation is also vital to performance, good physical conditioning at this stage will form the base for other performance factors developed during the planned 'Work' periods.

Like a pyramid, the bigger the base in training, the higher the peak can be. For Olympic competition, inevitably the base will be years in development rather than the six or seven months suggested here. Most importantly, this background training permits you to train harder during the Work 1 period because you will be fitter. If you slack off completely in winter, it's much harder to regain fitness, and if the first minor regatta of the season is windy it's likely to be a real trial.

▶ **Work 1**

In this phase you begin to convert your general aerobic and strength conditioning into specific fitness for sailing. Thus, your physical training becomes more specific, revolving mainly around practice for the particular demands of sailing your boat, such as hiking and trapezing. Consequently, spend more time sailing, developing technique, tactics and strategy. Also, progressively increase the training load (the number and intensity of practice sessions). For example, you could increase the number of training sessions per week from three to seven over a period of eight weeks. Initially this extra load on the body may cause performance to fall. But soon, your body will adapt to a higher level of conditioning, with a consequent improvement in performance.

▶ Peak 1

The aim here is to bring your physical performance to a peak. This occurs almost naturally when the intensity and duration of your workouts decrease following hard training. A taper is simply the period lasting from a few days to a few weeks before a competition where the training load is progressively reduced. As a result, the body becomes recharged. At this stage of the year, one to two months before your major competition, you can choose a minor regatta to sail and use your performance in this regatta to judge whether your training is on course. As well as providing experience for preparing properly for Peak 2, a well-planned physical and mental lead-up to the first competition will make the regatta a success – even if you don't win.

With a successful taper, you'll be sailing faster and feel great in the boat. The benefits of months of training will really start to show. This is because you finally get a good chance to recover and regenerate parts of the body that were often fatigued or run-down during consistent training.

• How to Taper Well and Peak for Competition

Ideally, you want to reach a peak in your physical and mental readiness in time to compete in a major regatta. The last few weeks and days before the event are vital in helping you reap the highest reward from your training efforts. Importantly, your training tapers!

The appropriate length of a taper can depend on several factors: the duration and importance of the regatta, your current level of fitness, how well you've recovered from previous regattas and your experience with previous tapers.

As a guide, the windier the regatta is likely to be or the more important and physically tough it is, the longer the taper should be. One day of rest is sufficient for a smaller local regatta. Three days would be minimum for a big regatta, and a week is not too early to begin tapering. Swimmers and rowers may start tapering 10 to 14 days out and their training plan is modified for up to four weeks prior to the competition.

Probably the most important principle in tapering to a competition is to reduce the volume of exercise, but maintain the intensity of training.

Realise also that, because of the cumulative nature of training, no exercise you do in those final few days can contribute to increasing your fitness for that particular regatta – so get some rest. However, on-water practice will still be important to sharpen your skills. On the final few days before a big regatta go out for shorter and sharper sessions, for example, an hour of work on boat speed, starting and basic boat handling.

How will you prepare for your next big regatta? (Kiel Week regatta, Germany).

Scientific research has shown that you can maintain a level of fitness for several weeks doing only half the work it took to achieve that level in the first place. So it is better to be possibly under-trained and fresh for a competition rather than potentially over-trained and worn-out.

In the last four weeks before a competition a training plan might look like this:

Training Plan – Four Weeks to go

Weeks to go	Weekly training emphasis	Intensity	Volume
4	Recovery & low-intensity, medium volume training (longer sailing sessions and aerobic exercise)	Low-Med	Medium
3	High intensity, low volume training (short, fast races)	High	Low
2	Lead-up competition or competition-specific training	High	Medium-Low
1	Limited competition-specific training and rest	Medium-High	Low
0	Sail well!		

In the above example, the intensity of training is more emphasised than the volume (hours) of training. This ensures specific and high-quality lead-up training is done in preparation for the racing at the end of the taper.

If we narrow down further, the final week's taper might look like that in the following table. Note that a reduction in the volume of training sessions is best to maintain the quality in your performance and ensure that your body is fully recovered.

Training Plan – Seven Days to go

Days to go	Activity	Intensity %	Volume (hr:min)
7	Racing – last day of a warm-up regatta	100	3:00
6	Sail – specific racing	95	0:45
5	Cycle/weights	80	1:00
4	Sail – reaching, strategy	85	1:30
3	Sail – speed, starts/rest	50 - 100	1:45
2	Sail 1 hour – short races (stretch)	50 (100 when racing)	1:00
1	Rest and little activity/stretch	Low	0:30
0	First race	100 (if windy!)	

During regular training it's also important to keep a day-to-day eye on the weather forecast. You may need to cancel or add training sessions depending on the wind.

But, how can you successfully taper for the first windy race of the regatta? Which races will be windy? I thought I was well prepared with one of my best tapers for a Pre-Olympic regatta. However, a hurricane blew in cancelling the first and then the second day of the regatta, leaving me feeling great but without any races to sail. When the regatta finally started, I felt an advantage had been lost. So if you're planning a serious taper, keep a good watch on the weather maps and the likely wind conditions on the first day of the regatta and prepare to be flexible.

Remember that the above information refers mainly to raw physical fitness. There are other important aspects of your total training regime that mustn't be forgotten in the final few days. For example, there is the importance of testing the water at a new regatta venue, refining skills, mental preparation, boat preparation, and so on. Arrange these areas to fit in with the physical preparation plan.

▶ Work 2

OK, back to the plan: You should have seen the benefits of a professional training plan by achieving a personal best in the minor regatta, now it's time to consolidate your training by using the fitness you developed to train even harder and take yourself to the next level!

End-year Training Plan

Chart showing Relative Performance Level over Months 10-12, with labels: Work 2 (1 month), Peak 2 (10 days), Major Regatta, Rest, Transition, Rest & Next year.

The Work 2 period should involve highly specific training with special attention to fitness and sailing skills, so on-water training is a priority. You can use the lessons learnt in the minor regatta to identify your weaknesses and develop a final four to five week plan which targets and eliminates the impact of these flaws on your sailing performance.

In this period before competition the intensity of training is increased with an accompanying reduction in training volume. Instead of endless hours of on-water training, you would turn to quality sessions that train all the sailing skills. Ideally, this will involve practice races against all the local hotshots you can muster. If they've read this book, they should be looking for you for the same reason!

▶ Peak 2

Dare I say it – this is the easy part! This is the final period before the major competition of the year and a natural outcome from months of work and a well-planned program. With the taper in training your body reaches a new high in physical development – you look and feel great and your confidence to sail well in the major regatta is only exceeded by your on-water ability.

The peak can include lead-up competitions that fine-tune your sailing skills. Mental preparation for competition is also important at this stage. Some of the time you usually spend physically training can now be used to think about the upcoming competition and summon a mental focus that will allow you to concentrate solely on the right things at the right time. For instance, time can be spent thinking about and imagining good strategy and tactics in the bigger and faster fleets you're likely to encounter.

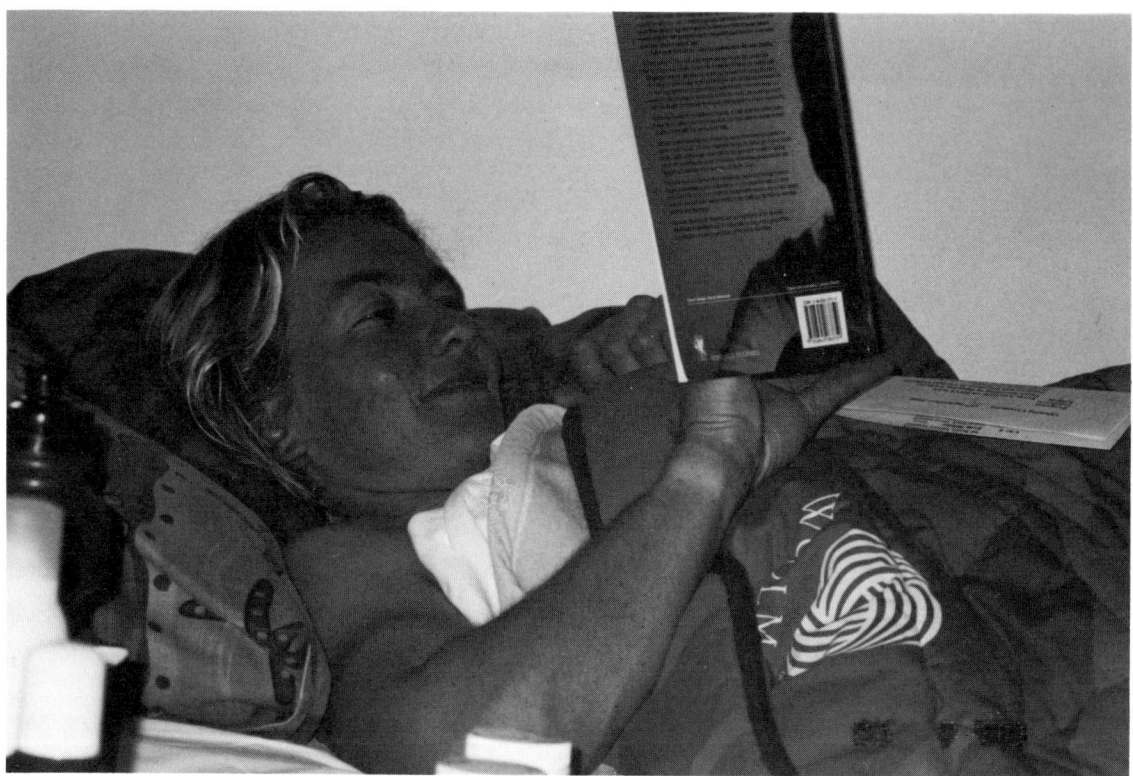

Motivational reading before a big competition.

▶Transition Phase

Take a break after your big competition. To ease away from the stress and strain of your most important regatta, it's recommended you cease serious sailing for one to four weeks. At the same time keep active – play soccer, tennis, touch football, water polo – so that you start the next year at a higher level of physical conditioning. This is how you can help to be sure that your performance will gradually improve each year. Thus, over the four years leading up to an Olympic regatta the increase in performance will look like the chart below and you'll have neared your personal best!

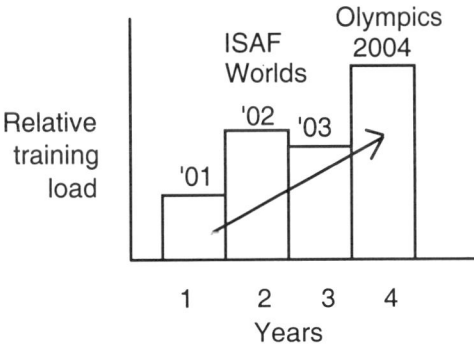

It is interesting that over the period of a week a good training load will follow a similar pattern to that above for an Olympiad or a single year. The gradual undulation in the intensity and volume of training can be programmed over a 7 to 10 day period as shown below. Using rest and recovery days allows the body to bounce back from harder periods of training and reduces the risk of illness from overtraining but still ensures an improvement in physical performance.

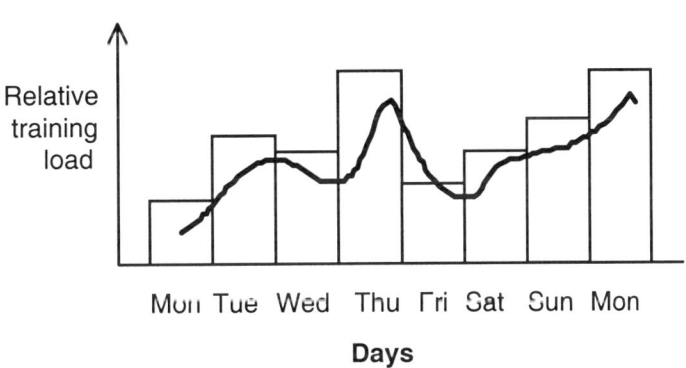

It takes a lot of self-control and determination to plan and carry out your 12-month plan. At the same time as providing solid goals to shoot towards, the plan must remain flexible to accommodate injury or illness and over or under-achievement of goals. Training need not be all go-go-go as there are definite times for taking it easy, plus times for driving hard – hence the bumpiness of the chart.

A similar plan to that illustrated was followed by the eventual 2000 gold medallists in the men's 470 from Australia – in what turned out to be a true underdog story. Discouraged by a 23rd place finish at the 1996 Olympics, Tom King, his crew Mark Turnbull and coach Victor Kovalenko set out in 1997 on what seemed like an exhausting training program. The team clocked up a thousand or more on-water hours in the form of planned work, taper and rest phases. This ensured improvement without bringing on mental and physical fatigue.

Gradually, over months and months, performance steadily improved. They finished 8th in the 1999 Worlds. They started winning multiple regattas the next year, including the 2000 World Titles. The pressure was then on them for the Games. However, they were safe in the fact that their extensive background training and preparation endowed them with the skills to handle their greatest challenge.

Of course not all sailors have a regatta program which will mimic the pattern of work and taper periods illustrated. Thus, some creative planning may be needed to establish a training formula that is suitable for regatta programs involving more than two proper 'peaks'. However, this should not prove too difficult as you will know future regatta dates, and can plan accordingly. The key is to first establish which regattas are a priority – choose up to three regattas per year – find out the dates they're on and work backwards to the present day.

▶▶9. RECOVERY – REVIVE AND SURVIVE

A single bout of very hard exercise, such as a long windy race, can depress the immune system for about 24 hours and particularly so in the first few hours after exercise. In this time the body is more susceptible to infectious agents like viruses of the throat and stomach – keep away from people with coughs and colds. These colds and stomach complaints may only last a day or two but are no good for continued training, competition or work. Recovering well from training can help you avoid such illness.

The immune system has two important roles during recovery from exercise: to protect the body against infectious agents and to help repair muscle and other tissue damaged during exercise. Too much exercise during recovery or returning too soon after injury or illness may slow the return of the body to full strength. What's more, continued heavy exercise may result in suppression of the immune system and an increased risk of illness. However, steps can be taken to minimise the risk of getting sick by planning training sensibly as well as by using recovery techniques during training and competition.

Go fly a kite: Light physical activity can help your body recover faster.

Recovery takes place in the time after you finish exercise until you start again and occupies by far the majority of an athlete's time. Importantly, the quicker you recover, the sooner you can train effectively again and increase your fitness further. Top athletes in the physically toughest sports like swimming and running may do four training sessions a day, however, two of these would be recovery sessions like plunging into hot and cool water, full-body massages or just light exercise.

Whether you're training heavily, competing in a long regatta or are regularly stressed-out you need to help the body and the immune system recover to avoid sickness and poor performance. Physical training is a 'dose-response' thing – do little and there are little benefits; do enough and the benefits are great; however, do too much and risk overtraining, burnout and sickness. More physical training is not always better because heavy exercise depletes the body's natural defence systems. The good news is that a moderate level of training will boost immunity. Recovering well can be the key to completing the maximum amount of training or surviving a tough competition without suffering too much from the stress the body goes through.

After a windy race or other form of heavy exercise the priorities for recovery are to eat, drink and stretch. In practice, these priorities might be combined with post-exercise activities shown in the Recovery table below.

Procedures to enhance your recovery

Activity	Recovery practices	When
Training or competition	Activity as per program, assuming all is well	
Cool-down	Drink (carbohydrate drinks)	During sail in/when you hit shore
	Light activity	Packing up gear
	Eat (very high carbohydrate)	15 to 30 min post-exercise
	Stretching – legs, shoulders, hips, back	As soon as practical
Post-session activities	Showers/spa/bath (include stretches)	30 to 60 min after exercise: 2 lots of warm for 3 min, cool for 30 sec – finish with cool
	Drink	30 to 60 min after exercise
End-day activities	Eat	As convenient/appropriate
	Ice pack – apply to sore areas	For 10 min each hour if needed
	Relaxation techniques (imagery, music, etc)	For 15 to 30 min
	Sleep (regular pattern)	For 8 hours minimum

Warm and cold showers, spas, saunas and massage act to stimulate the circulation. Heat and warm water encourage the blood vessels to open and increase blood flow around the surface of the body. In cold water, blood vessels closer to the skin constrict, thereby changing the distribution of blood flow within the body. Massage also encourages blood flow through the muscles. Together, the above techniques go some way to flushing out waste products in the muscles that are produced during exercise.

These warm applications (spas, saunas and massage) are often easy to do and just plain feel good when you are pooped. But personally, I also think that the application of cold can be better for you, especially to reduce muscle soreness.

I recommend having an ice pack handy in your freezer. Wrap the pack in a thin towel and apply it to your body's sore spots for 10 minutes as necessary. The cold will relax the muscles, reduce the sensation of pain and decrease inflammation. The net result might be that the part will recover to full strength faster.

Another alternative is to part-fill a bath with cold water, maybe adding some ice if you up for it (and considering room temperature), then lay in there for five minutes. Oh, the relief when you get out!

Cold appears to be effective and harmless and few complications or side effects after the use of cold therapy are reported. However, prolonged application at very low temperatures should be avoided as this may cause serious side effects, such as frostbite and nerve injuries.

Your resting heart rate recorded each morning just after you wake up may indicate whether your body has recovered well enough from recent training. As a rough guide, if your heart rate is five or more beats per minute above normal (recorded over 60 seconds) it may be better to do just light training or have a rest day. You can establish your 'normal' resting heart rate by recording it each morning for a week and taking the average of the three lowest readings. Note that resting heart rate can decrease as your aerobic fitness improves.

My heart rate was about 10 beats above normal early one morning the day after a couple of windy heats of a Laser World Titles. I wasn't quite sure whether my body wasn't completely recovered from the previous day or there was a little nervousness showing. So, I had some time before the next race to drink more (since dehydration increases the heart rate) and relax, listening to some favourite music. I'm sure this improved my chances in that day's racing as my results were as good as other days when I woke up in better condition.

Once you get to know your body and how well it normally recovers from regular training you will become more expert and be able to judge whether you should train with full intensity just from 'how you feel'. For instance, a rapid heart rate, lethargy, light-headedness, dizziness, muscle soreness and a dry throat may tell you to take a day off. Then again, it may be better to try to avoid such conditions by using a weekly training log to record the duration and intensity of training sessions and then rate the overall training intensity on a scale such as 1 (easy) to 7 (very hard). Always look back over the log to check that the overall intensity undulates on a weekly basis and that there aren't too many hard days in a row.

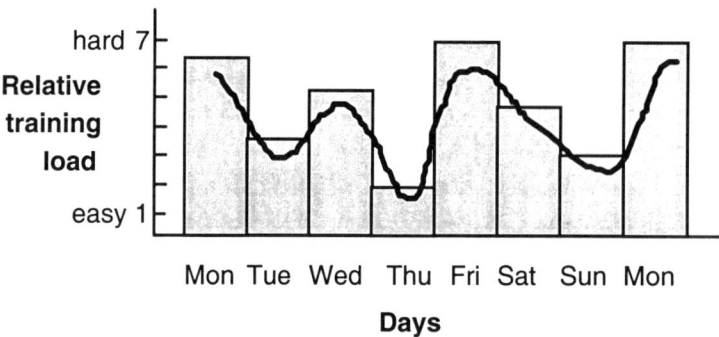

Your training load should undulate to allow recovery and gains in health and fitness.

When it's better not to train physically remember that you can still do effective training – try relaxation techniques, imagery and other forms of *mental* training. For example, there are a range of computer simulations of sailing available which can be used to practice tactics and strategy on your days off. Or, you could listen to your own audiotape that takes you through the thoughts and feelings of a sailing race.

The table below summarises the main types of recovery activities available. Recovery will be fast when the different recovery practices are used together. In particular, remember that light exercise, like a gentle swim or walk, is one of the best recovery tactics.

Summary: Ways to Recover Faster

Physical	Work/rest ratios (including active recovery – light exercise), ice packs, massage, stretching, physiotherapy, hot and cold showers, baths & spas.
Psychological	Relaxation, imagery, stress management.
Nutritional	High carbohydrate foods, balanced eating, supplements (in some cases).
Neurological	Sleep, rest, flotation.

▶▶ 10. EIGHT-WEEK TRAINING PROGRAM

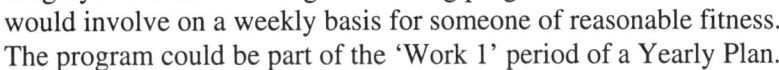

The sample eight-week training program below illustrates how the components of a training program discussed in this book might fit together. While people differ in the needs and aims of their physical training and therefore there is no single ideal training program for all people, this example roughly illustrates what a good training program would involve on a weekly basis for someone of reasonable fitness. The program could be part of the 'Work 1' period of a Yearly Plan.

The program is relatively compact and features two basic four-week periods. The first four weeks are for developing general fitness and so involve relatively more time cycling, swimming and weight training. The aim of the second four weeks are to enhance specific fitness, so more time is spent sailing and this is supplemented by cycling and weight-training sessions. Throughout the eight weeks, on-water training makes up the bulk of the program, from two-thirds to three-quarters of the training time per week.

Good improvements in fitness can be expected over the eight weeks and this can be monitored by completing the Home Fitness Tests (described in the next chapter) at the start and completion of the program.

▶ Notes on the Program

- Before each session complete a warm-up plus stretching.
- Between morning and afternoon sessions take a break of at least four hours.
- **Swim:** wearing flippers; 100m efforts - alternate 50m kicking (lying on back) with 50 m freestyle; 30 seconds rest between repetitions.
- **Gym – light:** follow the example for building muscle strength in the earlier section (Seven Top Sessions), but complete only two sets per exercise (30 to 40 minutes).
- **Gym – strength:** follow the strength example given earlier completely (approximately 60 minutes).
- **Gym – endurance:** follow the earlier example for building muscular endurance (45 to 60 minutes).
- **Cycle:** alternate between the cycling session examples in the earlier section (Seven Top Sessions).
- **Cycle/row session:** as described in Seven Top Sessions.
- **Sail:** a sample on-water session is given later in the section On-water Training.
- **Club race:** compete in the regular weekend races (allowing 2.5 hours).
- **Capital City Titles:** a chance to test your fitness and skill against some greater competition. (Four races, approximately 4.5 hours sailing each day).
- Space is provided to **record resting heart rate** (HR) during the harder weeks and if it is found to be too high, the program should be adjusted by substituting a rest or light activity day.
- **National Titles:** this is the targeted regatta, so greater rest is provided in the lead-up.

▶ Sample Training Program

Wks to go Intensity		Mon	Tue	Wed	Thu	Fri	Sat	Sun	Approx. Hours/ No. sessions
8-Light	a.m.			Cycle 0:45 min					
	p.m.		Gym – light		Gym – light		Club race	Club race	7:15 5
7-Medium	a.m.	Swim – 10x100m	Gym – light		Gym – Strength	Cycle 60 min			
	p.m.		Sail – 2 hrs				Club race	Club race	10:00 7
6-Hard	a.m.	Swim – 12x100m	Cycle – 60 min	Gym – strength			Massage		
	p.m.	Gym – strength		Sail – 2.5 hrs	Cycle 45 min hills		Club race	Club race	13:00 9
Resting HR									
5-Light	a.m.		Swim – 5x100m			Gym – strength		Cycle 60 min	
	p.m.	Gym – strength	Sail – 2 hrs				Club race	Club race	10:30 7
4-Hard	a.m.		Cycle – 45 min	Gym – strength			Capital city titles	Capital city titles	
	p.m.	Gym – strength	Sail – 2 hrs		Sail – 2 hrs				15:45 7
Resting HR									
3-Medium	a.m.			Gym – strength					
	p.m.	Cycl/row session	Sail – 2 hrs		Sail – 3 hrs	Gym – endurance	Club race	Club race	13:00 7
2-Med.-Hard	a.m.	Swim 10x100m		Cycle – 60 min	Massage				
	p.m.	Gym – strength	Sail – 2 hrs		Sail – 3 hrs	Gym – endurance	Club race	Club race	13:30 8
Resting HR									
1-Light	a.m.	Gym – endurance		Gym – endurance				Light cycle	
	p.m.		Sail – 2 hrs		Sail – 2 hrs		Club race		9:00 6
0-Racing	a.m.	Nationals						Rest	
	p.m.	Rest	Races 1&2	Races 3&4	Races 5&6	Races 7&8	Races 9&10		

▶▶ 11. HOME FITNESS TEST

It's often difficult to judge exactly how fit you are for sailing – you may be strong in some areas but weak in others. Below are five fitness tests you can use to more accurately judge your fitness for sailing. All the equipment you need is a set of weighing scales, a floor, a tape measure or ruler, a table and a wall.

These tests can be completed at regular intervals, for example every three months, so you can plot your progress and the change in fitness following training. Complete each test carefully, using a similar technique during a subsequent re-test to avoid deceitful results. Also, following a warm up, always complete the tests in the order listed so that any effects of fatigue from one test to the next are consistent.

▶ Body Weight

Measure your weight on an accurate set of scales while wearing minimal clothing and at a consistent time of day, for example, after waking up and going to the bathroom but before breakfast.

▶ Flexibility – Sit and Reach Test

Sit on the floor with the legs straight in front, no shoes, toes pointing up. Place one hand over the top of the other, fingertips overlapping and elbows straight. Then, lean forward as far as possible, sliding your hands towards or past your toes. The legs should remain straight and full stretch must be held for three seconds to avoid bouncing. The distance the fingers are from the soles of the feet is measured with a ruler (if the toes cannot be reached a negative score is recorded).

Targets

Club sailor	National level	International level
+6 cm	+12 cm	+18 cm

What the test measures. A general flexibility test that is also a practical test of the ability to lean in to adjust sail controls while hiking

What if you score low on this test? If you're not as supple as you could be your ability to move around the boat and into some of the awkward positions you sometimes need to adopt is limited. Note that if you're still growing, your bones may grow too fast for your muscles, leaving the muscles relatively short. So, in some cases, you may have poorer flexibility in adolescence compared with when you've finished growing. While females are generally more flexible than males, a lack of suppleness still needs to be worked on by both sexes. Greater flexibility is gained by stretching regularly before and after training.

▶ Abdominal Endurance

Lie on the floor with the knees bent up at 90 degrees and feet flat on the floor. Start with the arms straight, hands resting on top of the thighs, head on the floor. Then, slowly curl up so that the fingertips just touch the bottom of the kneecaps, and then curl back down with the head returning to the mat and hands sliding back to the starting position. Complete these crunches slowly and surely (one every three seconds) and record how many you can do. Correct form should be maintained and if any of the following occur stop the test: jerky movements (throwing the head, trunk or arms forward or letting the trunk fall to the mat); not sitting up far enough; not completing the repetitions at the prescribed rate; lifting the feet up from the floor.

Targets		
Club sailor	**National level**	**International level**
20 reps	50 reps	80 reps+

What the test measures. The abdominal muscles stabilise the trunk during hiking and many other activities during sailing, so this test measures the important ability of those muscles to work over an extended period.

What if you score low on this test? Poor abdominal endurance makes it harder to hike, trapeze and pump for extended periods and can put the health of your back at risk. Better do regular abdominal exercises to improve your endurance – see the following chapter on Lower Backs or turn to the Appendix for advanced abdominal exercises.

▶ Body-weight Pull-ups

Lie under a bar or edge of a table and rest your feet on the floor. With hands roughly shoulder width apart, pull your chest up to touch the bar or table and lower. Maintain strict form: your knees should remain bent at about 90 degrees; resist using your legs to help push; make sure your repetitions are full.

Targets		
Club sailor	**National level**	**International level**
10 reps	20 reps	30 reps+

What the test measures. This tests the strength of the arm and back muscles and can indicate your sheeting or pumping ability.

What if you score low on this test? Muscle strength is best improved by doing weight training or similar exercises. Turn back to Seven Favourite Training Sessions for examples of these. Developing greater strength in your upper body will make sheeting the sails and adjusting the sail controls easier.

▶ Wall-sit

Take up a position with your back against a solid wall with knees bent at 90 degrees (thigh horizontal and calf vertical). Wear shoes. The hands should be folded in front. Record how long you can hold this position (maximum 15 minutes). Be strict about maintaining a 90-degree knee angle.

Targets		
Club sailor	**National level**	**International level**
3 min	5 min	15 min+

What the test measures. This is a test of your ability to hold static muscle contractions of the thigh muscles, which makes it a measure of your hiking endurance.

What if you score low on this test? More hiking-like training may be needed. Remember that the static muscle work in hiking makes it quite different from most other forms of exercise, so the more specific training you do the better. As with hiking, this test can really hurt. But, also like hiking, your endurance can be increased by occasionally swapping the load from one leg to the other to encourage blood flow through the muscles.

▶ Practical Aerobic Test – Personal Time Trial

There is no specific equipment for this test – it's up to you. What's important is that you choose a mode of exercise to use to test yourself – cycling, running or swimming. Like a time trial, set yourself a distance to cover and complete it in the shortest possible time. Make the trial long enough to last between about five and 30 minutes.

Obviously, I cannot offer a specific target to achieve. However, once you have completed this trial a couple of times you can set yourself a goal for the longer-term. Or, race against your crew.

What the test measures. This is a test of your aerobic ability, i.e., your general endurance and ability to sustain exercise over an extended period.

What if you fail to improve on this test? It may be that you were already super-fit. However, more often than not it would mean you could consider increasing the frequency and/or intensity of your aerobic training.

▶▶ 12. AVOIDING INJURY

Sailing isn't a body contact sport, and water offers a soft landing, so sailors seldom arrive home on crutches – unlike footballers, basketballers and cyclists (and board sailors too sometimes!). But there are plenty of other opportunities to injure yourself, ranging from a minor collision with a misplaced fitting, to sunburn-induced skin-cancer. Avoiding injury is vital so that your training is not interrupted and nothing stops you from sailing your boat well.

Some injuries are sheer nuisance value – they slow you down and spoil your fun – but other more serious problems can develop over time: don't let them.

Heat, cold, sun and wet clothes are common causes of skin problems. Ultraviolet radiation from glare, salt water and squinting can cause eyestrain. You've probably found that problems develop from little things you don't notice at first – your eyes don't focus as well when you're fatigued, for instance; muscle soreness and back pain creep up on you, and you're more likely to be hit by a swinging boom when you tire and start to lose concentration, or when the wind you thought you wanted, arrives. Then there are the spectacular one-offs you can do without – such as an elbow whacked by the bow of a planing boat at a gybe mark or being flung into the mast from a nosedive while on trapeze.

▶ Eyes

The eyes can often be a source of pain after a long day on the water – the tired, dry and scratchy feeling. Wearing sunglasses can help avoid these symptoms and at the same cut long-term exposure to UV rays that are damaging to the eyes. The common, but unpronounceable pterygium is a cloudy growth on the surface of the eye that can block vision by slowly growing across the pupil. The primary cause of pterygium is ultraviolet (UV) light, which reflects off the sails and water.

Some years ago it was reported that as many as 50 per cent of U.S. Olympic hopefuls reported they had pterygium. I've also had one for eight years and luckily it hasn't grown. (Pterygiums are also common in surfers who are also exposed to sun and salt water for long periods).

Surgery temporarily corrects the problem, but after removal by surgery there is more chance of re-growth and it may be only a matter of months before the surgery may need to be repeated. Sailors with pterygium (and those wanting to avoid it) really need a peaked hat and sunglasses filtering 100 per cent of UV rays.

However, it is unfortunate that the eyes offer so much useful information while sailing and so we often prefer to keep the eyes uncovered while racing. Still, sunglasses can be worn up to the start and after finishing for the ride in. This can help the eyes function better during racing since their ability to recover after exposure to glare will gradually decrease the more time we spend looking at dazzling water and sails. It may take more than 24 hours for the eyes to get their glare recovery ability back after constant exposure, so the less time squinting at bright objects the better.

▶ Skin - Sun

Australians in particular enjoy an afternoon of fun and sun and it shows in the statistic that Australia has the highest incidence of skin cancer in the world. Anti-cancer bodies recommend against suntan. As they advise, *Slip* (on a long-sleeved top), *Slop* (on 30+ sun screen 20 minutes going into the sun) and *Slap* (on a peaked hat) is obviously the way to go. However, often we're out there for longer than expected without everything covered up, the 30+ washes off, we can't see wind shifts with sunnies on and get burnt.

To achieve effective skin protection, hats and clothing should be the first choice for sailors. Sunscreen should be applied to the areas we can't hide from the sun, when the skin is dry. Shop carefully for a sunscreen that is water-resistant for four hours. Many sailors also carry a small stick or bottle of cream with them to apply between races when on the water for a long time. A small sunscreen stick is also ideal as it is easy to store, and water resistant. Zinc cream can be used to avoid the wash-off problem in some areas such as the nose, ears and lips but you shouldn't use zinc on large areas because it may stop the skin sweating and stop the body cooling itself naturally on a frustrating light-wind day.

▶ Foreign Bodies

Parts on a small boat can be identified as 'danger areas'; for example, scrapes and cuts may occur from the sharp edge of a bolt or screw that is not flush with the fitting. Then there are the areas of a boat where a hand or foot can get caught just at the time you need it somewhere else and in the quick pullout, damage is done. Modifying fittings or promising to stay clear of parts of your boat that are menacing may avoid some such injuries.

Sailors and board sailors alike also report suffering marine stings, blisters, ear infection, knee injury, and splinters. Again, many of these injuries can often be prevented by preparation – wearing correct fitting booties or shoes, wearing a wetsuit and gloves, using ear drops and avoiding heavy wind and waves when inexperienced.

Sailing injuries other than those that are sun-related are more likely to occur when the wind is up. Everything is speeded up when it's blowing – tacks, gybes, capsizes – so the potential for something to come

Slopping on sunscreen.

flying into you or for you to go flying into some part of the boat (the gunwale, centreboard, ratchet block, etc.) is greater. For example, in high winds, the boom vang may be strapped tighter, leaving a smaller gap to slot under during a tack. Remembering to duck a little lower (and being agile) can prevent a bump on the head or a nasty swipe across the back by a fitting on the boom that hangs down. If you do suffer an injury like a bruise or muscle strain, then the first priority in most cases is to apply an ice pack to the area as soon as possible so that the injury recovers faster.

▶Cuts and Abrasions

A small cut to a sailor's skin can be a real problem because the injury is often roughed up again if you're out sailing before the skin seals itself. If the wound remains open for a long time it can become seriously infected and cause overall body sickness.

There is a simple procedure to take care of small wounds. When possible, it is important to rinse with tap water and apply a povidone-iodine solution (eg, Betadine) to the surface for 4-5 minutes. The wound will need further (Doctor) treatment if it is still bleeding, gaping or more than one centimetre long. If the wound is damp after sailing and you can keep it clean for a few hours, leave it open so it can dry out.

If you need to continue to race or train then you need to apply a waterproof dressing. This dressing, a clear polyurethane film, available at a pharmacy, should be cut to extend beyond the wound by about 3 cm. You may need to shave the area to ensure the dressing sticks well. The dressing can be left on for days or until the wound is nearly closed. An excess of white fluid can be seen under the dressing during healing - this is fine. You must add a cover to the dressing if the area is subject to further abrasion. For example, cover with a small cloth then wrap with tape or stretch a wide elastic band over the area.

Poor nutrition can be a factor in the healing of wounds. If your diet is poor, supplementation with vitamins A, C, E plus iron, zinc and magnesium may be necessary.

▶Fitness and Avoiding Injury

Good preparation for sailing also involves getting your body prepared for the physical demands of the sport. Aerobic exercise and weight training can help prevent injury by building-up the strength of all the joints and stop you getting tired so quickly and fall over in the boat and being bruised, or whatever.

It seems fitness can even help you overcome the adverse effects of bumps and bruises we all get at some stage on the water. Past world champion Glenn Bourke knows (reported in *Championship Laser Racing*): once before the start of a major race he suffered a heavy bump

There is a greater potential for injury on windy days.

to a knee, effectively preventing him from hiking off that leg. He started the race hiking on one leg and to his wonder found his leg endurance good enough to reach the top mark in reasonable shape. Gradually during the race, full function returned to the bumped knee, allowing him to hike fully by the finish.

Glenn goes on to say that this ability to break through such pain can be an important mental aid to performance, such as when struggling up the last beat of the third windy race in a day. True enough, but obviously Glenn can read his body well and knows when the presence of pain means he is working hard or there is just a temporary hurt and what sort of pain is telling him there is something seriously wrong with his body and he should stop and pay attention to it.

Top marathon runners also have a great ability to read their bodies during races. They are alert for signals as to when all is well and they can make a surge or when, for example, the first signs of an injury are appearing because of poor running technique. Conscious of their body's feelings during exercise, they spot signs of a problem early and adjust pace or technique to the optimum. As a result, they can reach the finish line or the end of a training session with just about all their energy expended and largely avoid injury that would slow them down in the long term.

▶▶13. DRESSED FOR SUCCESS – SAILING CLOTHING

Sailing is generally pleasant, but there are also many times when it's not as comfortable as our non-sailing friends believe. I'm a firm believer that the more comfy you are when sailing the more fun you'll have and the easier it will be to sail the boat well.

By comfortable, I mean not experiencing all the things that make it uncomfortable - gunwale bum, sunburn, rope burn, wetsuit rashes, cold and wet, bruises, and so on. Sailing may never be quite like lying in a warm bed in the morning when it's cold and raining outside but there are many great experiences to be had sailing in otherwise tough conditions. So, with the things that hurt in sailing in mind, lets examine some of the products and techniques that can make sailing more comfortable.

▶Keeping Warm When it's Cool

Mum always said wear many layers to keep the cold out. Thermal pants and jumpers from makers like Helly Hansen and Musto usually form one of the first layers close to the skin. The different brands vary in their construction and fabric, particularly in how much water they retain and their thickness.

In cool conditions you'd be wise to wear a couple of thermal jumpers under a good quality spray top or even a dry top. Look for a spray top with good, comfortable or adjustable seals around the wrists, neck and waist. It should feel relatively light to wear and allow a good range of movement. It may be lined and the seams glued to make it truly waterproof. If you are exercising hard, another, yet more expensive option is a breathable spray top. Sweat is less likely to build up under such a garment, making it more comfortable when the pressure is on.

A three-quarter leg or full-length wet suit is also a good investment so that you don't lose the heat that you're keeping in so well in your upper body. But as it gets colder, staying dry becomes more important.

Some of the coldest sailing I've done was at a regatta in the South of France in an early European spring. On one of the days there was a light but steady breeze with a persistent drizzle and temperature about six degrees. The Australian Laser sailors, who had never sailed in such cold weather, put on all the sailing clothes they brought with them before heading out for the three races. I shivered the whole way around the course in the first race in my short wetsuit, three thermals and spray top.

The following races were delayed for a while and all around sailors were doing push ups, jumping up and down and swinging their arms around in a vain attempt to combat the cold. By that stage I was shivering more and decided to pull out of the two remaining races. I was still shivering after a 20-minute hot shower and having put all my dry clothes on. The other Aussies later came in with numb fingers and were very, very cold. Before racing the next day we went shopping. How much for a dry suit? $500. Ok, we'll take four!

With rubber seals around the neck, ankles and wrists, a dry suit is designed to keep out all water. So you can put on warm, dry clothes and the dry suit over the top and you're fine when it's less than 10 degrees. However, when the wind comes up and you start sweating, all your dry clothes get wet anyway, reducing the effectiveness of the set-up.

Since you lose a lot of heat through your head, another good investment for the cold is a wet-suit hat, a beanie or a balaclava.

If you put all the above together, on the 'average winter day' in southern Australia or spring in Europe or parts of the US you could be warm enough wearing a long wetsuit, two thermal jumpers, a good spray jacket, boots and socks, gloves, a personal flotation device (life jacket) and a beanie.

As a guide, make sure that the clothing you're wearing makes you toasty before you leave the beach, considering that getting wet will cool you down slightly. I think it is also good to accept being slightly cold before the race, so when you start exercising hard during the race, the extra heat you generate doesn't make you too hot. Sailboarders and any crew working hard will have more trouble deciding how much to wear. If possible, I think it is best to avoid wearing too many clothes during the race and to have a big jacket and warm head wear available on a coach or rescue boat for between races.

▶ Don't Get Beat Up

When someone showed me the new wetsuit he had designed with an extra layer over the bottom I baulked at his lack of tolerance for gunwale bum. You know, the rash and irritation from clothes rubbing across a wet bottom that in turns rubs across a rough deck. However, after wearing one of these wet suits with the super-padded posterior for a number of seasons I now know it's one of the simplest and best ways to prevent a sore bum. (For these suits see: www.queensportmarine.com.au/home.htm. Other good sailing gear: http://www.hellyhansen.com).

You'd be wise to pad up your bottom before boating as well, either by adding to your existing shorts or trying one of the retail products available as gunwale bum must surely be one of the more trivial but common things that distracts us from the wind and sails. If the padding doesn't fix the problem, check the seams of your wetsuit or underwear. The less bulky the seams are the better. Wearing a pair of lycra bike pants under your wetsuit can also eliminate irritation from these seams.

When talking sailing gloves, grip and protection are two main concerns. Use traditional leather sailing gloves for protection but rubber ones for great grip. The former now come in cut-off and full-finger varieties to avoid the ride-down problem but require good care to keep them soft and functional.

Rubber dishwashing or gardening gloves are my choice for dinghy sailing. The main advantage of the rubber glove is that it virtually grips the rope by itself, requiring less grip strength than a bare hand or a leather sailing glove. However, they wear out quickly and it may take only 10 sails before they fall apart. But they are quite cheap compared to 'sailing gloves'.

I forgot my hat! Warm-weather (Dubai, UAE) gear includes hiking pants, rash top, life jacket and rubber sailing gloves.

Hiking can hurt in so many places - the instep of the feet, the front of the calves, under the thighs, in the thigh muscles, the hip muscles, the stomach muscles, the lower back... A lot of the discomfort is from the effort of the muscles and body during exercise. However, hiking can be made significantly more comfortable with the right clothing and equipment.

A high-density foam-padded hiking strap will help to spread the load over the instep of the feet and reduce the chance of bruising that area. The foam (or even wet suit material) must be solidly fastened to the hiking strap webbing - sewn or glued - and it's best that it is covered with a tough fabric.

Although hiking boots often feel clumsy when moving around the boat and seemingly tie ropes around themselves, their useful functions can outweigh these deficiencies. Number one, they reduce the chance of cutting your feet on the boat ramp or in shallow water. Two, they reduce the physical wear to the instep of your feet from the hiking strap and help grip the deck. And three, they help to keep your feet pointed toes-up when hiking, lessening the load on some of the calf muscles so you may be able to hike longer, or harder. Ankle support is best with less-flexible lace-up boots, such as Aigle, Burke and Douglas Gill varieties.

You can appreciate that having a good rubberised grip on the sole of the boot is invaluable when moving around the boat. Sailboarders in particular need a light-weight bootie that fastens securely to the foot and grips the deck like a magnet.

Another thing I have noticed is that the surface on the top (instep) of the boot is also quite important. Some boots naturally grip the hiking strap well, reducing the effort on your part. Others slip and slide along the strap, making it hard to keep a firm footing.

Battened hiking pants have been a real boon as they reduce bruising to back of the thighs and lower the overall load on the thigh muscles when hiking, allowing the determined to hike better. Make sure they're not too lose (or they will move around when hiking) or too tight (or they will restrict blood flow and rub) and that the straps over the shoulder are well adjusted for your height.

If you often get a tight neck and shoulders when sailing, have a look at how tight your clothes pull down on your shoulders. A wet suit that is too short or that has very tight shoulder straps can elicit a slight tension in the neck and shoulder muscles that can gradually become irritating and cause you to slump. Try loosening the straps off or getting a better-fitting wetsuit so you can sit up straight.

For trapeze crews, a long wetsuit is often necessary to help avoid heavy bruising of the shins through collisions with parts of the boat.

▶ Be Cool when it's Hot and Wet

Sailing in warm to hot weather is as breezy as it gets. You can cut back on bulky jumpers, wetsuits and spray jackets and don't mind a few buckets of fresh seawater in the face.

As mentioned, one thing that is important in the heat and glare of a summer day is taking care of your eyes. They can only take a certain amount of bright light and glare off the water before their ability to re-adjust becomes affected. Wear sunglasses at least before and after racing. Of course, avoid sunburn to the rest of your body as well with a rash shirt, hat and sunscreen.

Warm weather usually offers the most pleasant sailing conditions since you can get away with wearing the minimum. For very hot conditions a hiking-pants manufacturer developed a short hiking pant with a stretchy mesh covering for the front of the thighs. These were great as they allowed water to wash over the part of the thighs that were working the hardest, keeping them cooler than the normal suit.

Maybe the best advice on keeping cool when it's hot is to use the water you're floating on! It will cool the body 100 times more effectively than the same temperature air, so splash yourself and wet your clothing before and between races to keep your body's temperature down. To properly lower your body temperature, leave whole parts of your body in the water for a minimum of five minutes.

If you need to go to the toilet three times a night or more, then adding a little salt to foods or your drinks will help maintain hydration in hot weather. Check your urine colour and volume regularly - a fluorescent or deep yellow colour and little output is a good sign you need a top up of 200-500mls immediately and more later.

Water everywhere and nothing to drink? Please no. Carry a water bottle (with your favourite drink) on board to refresh that dry mouth and keep your body hydrated.

Colder: Beanie, thermal jumpers, longer wetsuit and spray jacket (Copenhagen, Denmark).

Clothing for warm sailing and additional gear that may be needed for cool and icy sailing.

Warm	Mild	Cold
Wetsuit or hiking pants	Thermal jumper	Dry suit
Rash shirt	Spray jacket	Thermal pants
Footwear	Long wet-suit	Beanie or balaclava
Socks?		
Swim costume		
Gloves		
Hat		

▶ The Personal Flotation Device

The Personal Floatation Device (and the other names used around the world for a buoyancy aid or life jacket) is a bulky but essential item of sailing clothing. However, it is not really thought of much after the initial purchase, just put it on and go sailing. But before that initial purchase, think about style and function - what's really necessary, what's comfortable and what the rules say you must wear.

I think the aim for the racing sailor is to have the smallest and least bulky PFD possible for your body weight. Put a small one on, make sure you can take a full breath and can swing your arms, twist around freely and the like and I think you've got the right size.

A tighter buoyancy vest has less chance of catching on part of the boat, such as the boom during a tack. Also, if you choose one that hugs you like a bear it will work better in the water, reducing drag when swimming and of course, providing effective buoyancy. Avoid a vest that wants to ride up around the neck as it won't keep you afloat properly and will become annoying while sailing.

To be worn with a trapeze harness, the vest must be short to the waist so the hook is clear. A popular style is one that sashes over the head and has a Velcro adjustment around the lower chest.

To go racing with a new PFD you should check that it meets the safety requirements for the regatta, for example, in Australia AS1512 on the vest's label is acceptable. Other countries have different regulations; the Racing Rules require that the PFD be adequate for the conditions.

A good additional feature to your PFD is a small mesh pocket or pouch, Velcro sealed. They can be handy for a spare protest flag, sunscreen stick or food bar.

▶▶14. LOWER BACKS – THE STAYED BACK

Back pain is common to many small boat sailors who are at it for extended periods, and there is a lot that can be done to avoid a bad back.

The spine is really a kind of mast (one of those new bendy rigs!) that holds the head and arms up and allows the transfer of force between the upper and lower limbs. The abdominal and back muscles and other bits (ligaments and tendons) act as stays, bracing and also helping to move the spine.

It's a very complex arrangement of equipment and it's often heavily loaded. With most things of this nature, the lower back has its fair share of problems. Ranging from the infrequent niggly muscle spasm to the immense-sounding *spondylolisthesis* where the vertebrae become miss-aligned, about 80 per cent of people have at least one disabling bout of back pain at sometime.

Some of the things we do while sailing directly impact on lower back function and can lead to injury and chronic discomfort. For example, sitting with the trunk twisted to look forward can cause muscle spasms that can be painful but can also be stretched out after a race. A bad back may not slow us down as much as some injuries – the pain can often go away when exercising anyway. However, there may be serious long-term consequences and it would probably be better if it weren't there to distract you or limit your range of movement.

Lower back injuries are often due to weak muscles around the spine, imbalances in the strength of muscles that work against one another and the stress placed on the spine by the nature of the sport – hiking, trapezing, pumping and sitting unsupported. Doing all these required twisting and jerking movements, would be a leading contributor to low back pain by straining the joints. However, there are many causes and different reasons for lower back pain so you should seek medical advice to find a cure or relief for your exact cause. The focus here is on general points about spine pain together with proven tips on how to help improve the general condition of your back.

▶Hiking Muscles

'Ugh, gee that must hurt!' is a common remark from non-sailors seeing someone hiking close-up for the first time. The hiking diagram helps show where low back pain might come from while hiking. The hip flexor muscles (1), connected to the top of the legs and the lower back, hold the torso up. The abdominal muscles (2) act to prevent the back arching whenever the hip muscles work (like a backstay) – that's most of the time when hiking. Problems occur when the abdominals are not strong enough or become fatigued during a race or you lean back too far (beyond about a 150° angle between the leg and trunk). In each case the hip muscles have to work harder to hold the trunk up, and there is a tendency to arch the back.

Good abdominal muscles are important for your hiking posture

Healthy abdominal muscles

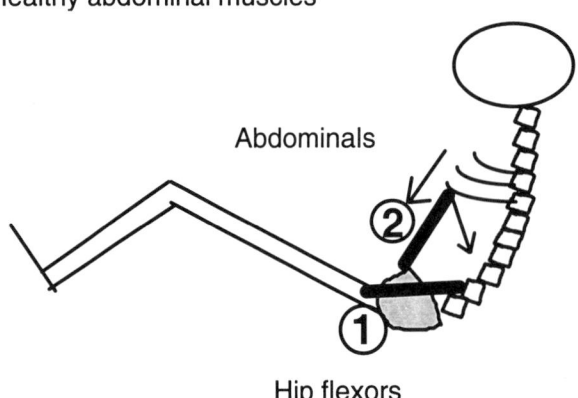

Weak abdominals, leaning back too far

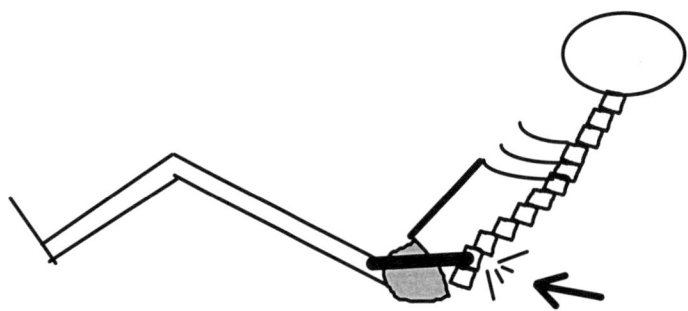

On a similar note, you've probably heard of the idea not to do sit-ups with the legs straight – the reason being that it causes the hip flexors to pull hard on the spine, making it arch. However, it is fair to say that it is safe to do straight-legged sit ups *if* the abdominal muscles are very strong, allowing you to curl up and down again while not arching the lower back. Sitting-up and hiking are similar (hiking is really where you're stuck in the middle of a sit-up) so all this suggests that sailors' abdominal muscles need to be strong to keep the lower back in shape.

Mention should also be made of the 'side-stays' – the muscles down the side of the trunk. These are just as useful as the main abdominal muscles for supporting the trunk and preventing the low back arching. These muscles are better trained by trunk-twisting and side-bending exercises rather than ordinary crunches or sit-ups – see below.

▶ Preventing Back Pain

Remember I mentioned strengthening and stretching earlier? Not only should you strengthen the abdominals but also stretch the hip flexors. Never when hiking are the hip flexors really stretched – only tensed – and this leaves them physically shorter. This shortening over a long time (weeks to months) can add to the low back arching. Thus, after hiking, stretches should be done of the hip flexors by opening the hip joint – moving the thigh back under the bottom.

Stretch of the hip and quadriceps muscles after a day on the water – keep the abdominals tight then slowly lift the foot until a stretch is felt.

That said, again I should warn that these exercises may not be useful if this is not the cause of your back pain. For instance, my back pain seems to come from a combination of things – muscle imbalances, slightly different leg lengths as well as (previously) weak abdominals and tight hip flexors. Different muscles need to be developed and or stretched for each of these causes.

So apart from understandable must-dos like bending the knees rather than the back when lifting boats, what can be done for a sailor's back? The following gentle range of motion and strengthening exercises are used to prevent and treat low back pain.

Pelvic Tilt. Lie on your back with knees bent, feet flat on the floor. Draw your tummy down, flattening the small of your back against the floor, without using the legs. Hold for 5 to 10 seconds.

Knee to shoulder. Lie on your back with your knees bent and feet flat on the floor. Grasp and slowly pull your right knee towards your shoulder and hold 5 to 10 seconds. Lower the knee and repeat with the other knee.

Prone press-up. Lie on your stomach, hands near your shoulders, as if to do a push-up. Slowly push your shoulders up, keeping your hips on the floor and letting your upper back then lower back and stomach sag. Slowly lower your shoulders back to the floor, letting the back curl down. Repeat five times.

While the above are simple rehabilitation exercises, the following target the typical weak points, strengthening the abdominals and back muscles and developing muscle coordination to help eliminate the factors that cause back pain.

Swiss ball exercises (See the Appendix for a complete description)
- Seated single leg
- Prone alternate arm and leg rise
- Swiss prone single leg off

Core exercises
- Crunches
- Toe-touch
- Side raises
- Forearm plank
- Back extension

The above range of exercises can be included as part of your gym program, usually done at the end of the session.

▶▶15. TRAVELLING IN A JET PLANE

▶Jet Lag

Fly across a number of time zones and you get jet lag because the body will no longer go to sleep and wake up at the same time. This disruption to your internal cycle of sleep and activity will take up to seven days to overcome, but you can be back to normal in 3-4 days by doing the following.

Set your watch to the new time zone when you sit down on the plane and behave as much as you can as though you are already in that time zone. For instance, be very restful and get some shut-eye if it is the middle of the night at your destination or stay awake longer if it is still morning in the country you're travelling to. Once you get there don't sleep before your normal bedtime.

Sunlight or other light appears to be the main signal the body uses as to what it should be doing. So, if sleepy in the morning, keep busy with menial tasks, maybe sightseeing and orientation, but whatever, keep your eyes open. Also, eat at normal meal times as soon as possible. Don't expect your physical performance to be up to scratch for a couple of days after landing, so avoid terribly exhaustive exercise.

▶Jet Stress

If you stay on an airplane for many hours, irrespective of whether you cross time zones, you will suffer jet-stress. This stress is from dehydration from the low humidity of the cabin, unusual food, lack of space and noise. These stressors can be minimised by using ear plugs, eye masks, getting up and moving around the cabin, regular drinking (except alcohol), and by using a damp cloth over the mouth and nose while sleeping.

> You can also use sugar-free chewing gum, lozenges or chewable vitamin C tablets to help keep your saliva flowing. Yes, drink regularly too.

I think it is especially important to avoid drying of the mouth and throat on a long flight. Often late in a flight, you hear people around the cabin start coughing because their throats have dried out and become irritating. It's important to keep the mouth and throat well hydrated because your saliva contains antibodies that provide an initial defence against disease. If the throat is dry, there is less natural defence available.

At stopovers, you may notice your feet and lower legs have swollen from extended sitting. To get this fluid back to the rest of your body, try lying on the floor of the transit lounge with your feet up on the chair. Then you'll really look like a seasoned traveller! On board, you should also move around the plane every 1-2 hours to stretch out a little and get the circulation going.

If you wind up in a much hotter or colder place than home then be wary that this can place extra stress on the body. Pay special attention to hydration when it's hot, making sure your urine is a light colour or clear. Of course, when it's colder keep warm, and try to avoid those who may have winter colds.

▶Avoiding sickness

Sometimes it seems easier to get sick when you're away from home. Exposure to different stresses and people who are already sick are major causes. A number of guidelines should be followed to avoid illness:

- Wash your hands before meals and after touching someone who is sick.
- Ensure all food has been freshly cooked.
- Avoid shellfish, salads (as they may be washed in contaminated local water), and fruits that can't be peeled.
- Avoid ice in drinks, brushing teeth with tap water and drinking tap water. Note that tap water in many countries may be safe but your body may just not be sufficiently used to all that is in the water to handle a lot of it.
- Boil water at least 10 min if no bottled water is available.
- Do not share drinking bottles; rinse them thoroughly with boiled water or the liquid you're drinking.
- Use insect repellents and try to stay in rooms with screens when staying in areas where mosquitoes spread disease.
- Do not share eating utensils, toothbrushes, razors, clothing, towels or share food with someone who is sick. This is important to prevent cross-infection of other members of a team.

▶▶16. FITNESS FOR YOUNG SAILORS

When you're 9-16 years old or so there can be other things that get in the way of having some good sailing races – especially school! There are a number of important points on fitness for youths in sailing.

This age range is all about having fun in the sport, playing at it but not being overly focused on strict training patterns. In fact, youths usually learn movement skills faster than adults and so it is important to develop quality sporting skills when young.

In learning skills, it is best and more effective if the child is taught efficient movements rather than learn totally by trial and error. Skills like tacking and gybing will also be better learned in controlled situations away from competition (flat water and light winds). Often, the focus is on the club race on the weekend and there is virtually no dedicated training time. Ideally, the athlete will find a good coach and a little spare time to work on skills.

It is interesting that early developers who specialise in one sport from an early age are likely to drop out as they are overtaken by later developing peers. Aiming to improve all the sailing skills and participation in other sports and activities will increase the chances of an early maturer continuing to be physically active.

There is little difference in strength between boys and girls before puberty, say to 12 years. Then, more rapid development occurs in the heart, lungs and muscles and in the teenage years there can be vast differences in children's strength, size and endurance. This makes it important to match the sailor's size to the class of boat so that the power to weight ratio ensures they can be competitive with other sailors in the class.

Sixteen and up, athletes may be introduced to well supervised strength training in the form of circuits and body-weight exercises. Any weight-training program should be undertaken with caution, especially if the athlete is still growing in height. There is the possibility that if the weights are too heavy, the technique is not correct or the repetitions are too great, that damage may be caused to the growth centres of the long bones of the athlete. Permanent damage to these areas could cause growth to cease in the bone.

A boy's flexibility can decrease more than a girl's with age, and some boys finish puberty with an extremely tight hamstring/lower back area (i.e., they can't get close to touching their toes). It's best to pick this up early and start regular stretching exercises after training while the joint and muscles are more malleable.

Below is a simple case study for a youth's training.

Case Study 1 – Belinda	
Subject:	15 years old, Height 1.66 cm, Weight 59kg, been sailing 5 years.
Sailing History:	Started in Optimist and now has a Laser Radial.
Goals:	Develop fitness and increase body weight for Radial; compete in Radial Worlds and ISAF Youth Worlds.
Sails:	2-3 days per week - Club races, regional regattas, national titles, extra days during school holidays.

Optimists are a beginning boat for thousands of sailors world-wide (and here in Suva, Fiji).

Belinda may yet grow a little taller; growth is usually finished by the age of 17 or so in girls. During puberty, the long bones can outgrow the muscles. This could impact on Belinda's **suppleness**, so now she needs to pay special attention to stretching exercises. She knows that the hamstring muscles in the back of the legs and the lower back are key areas to stretch given their role in hiking, reaching inboard while hiking and in general movement around the boat.

While she is still growing, Belinda should avoid heavy weight training exercises. This is because there are still weak areas in the joints, prone to injury from heavy loads. For life, she wants to stay nice and trim so she looks good. However, she also appreciates that she must put on a little weight for the Radial. She hopes she will grow tall enough to add weight without having to bulk up. Nonetheless, some resistance training can be useful to increase her functional **strength** and size.

She doesn't need barbells and dumbbells; her own body weight and some imagination are sufficient. Twice a week she does 20-30 minutes of push-ups, assisted chins-ups, body-weight pull-ups, body-weight squats, abdominal and lower back exercises. Her aim here is to broadly develop all of her body so it is ready for a professionally tailored strength program that she plans to start next year.

Developing **stamina** is a key focus for an athlete of this age. She cycles to school each day, a total of around 30 minutes a day, five days a week. She used to play hockey a couple of days a week, but now it's mainly sailing. She doesn't need extra hiking bench work at this stage as she usually gets enough windy sailing in her three sessions a week. Besides, her dad is only half way through building a hiking bench!

Belinda is proficient in most of the basic **skills** of sailing and now needs more technical input, good practice and refinement to continue to improve. Belinda gets in a few hours each week practicing in a non-competitive environment. She is also always thinking of questions to ask other sailors and is a keen observer of others' technique. She does five real sessions per week (although none are high-volume), up from the three she did up until she turned 15.

Belinda doesn't know much about sports psychology, mental **spirit** and the like. She just likes going sailing and racing. However, when asked what percentage of sailing performance is attributable to mental versus physical performance she admits that sailing is at least 50% mental. She is not really sure what to do for her head and vows to find out more about the subject.

Summary of average week's work	
Monday	Light cycle, Strength
Tuesday	Light cycle, Rest
Wednesday	Light cycle, Sail
Thursday	Light cycle, Strength
Friday	Light cycle, Rest
Saturday	Sail
Sunday	Sail

▶ Comments

Some days Belinda gets a bit tired. Her basic week, above, isn't that hard. It's the extra stuff she likes to do with her buddies - swimming, fun times late at night and the like. That's fine. She knows to take a rest day when she has over done it. But also, she knows that she only gets each day once to develop the fitness and skills she needs to reach her goals.

The commutes to school and home by bicycle are a good practical way to combine fitness training and necessary travel.

Hopefully, when it comes to the Radial worlds, it will be school holiday time. Then, she will have time beforehand to get in a little more on-water work, possibly in the form of a lead-up regatta. In a couple of years she wishes to move to the Europe class or maybe a 470 and go to the Worlds. In the meantime she must steadily learn as much as possible, making many mistakes and enjoying her racing. It takes a long time to get to the top in sailing, and with steady work she can gradually get there.

▶▶ 17. FITNESS FOR MASTERS SAILORS AND OLD SALTS

Sailing is a great life-long sport and certainly has a healthy masters involvement (over 35 years) – actually, healthy in numbers, but of a wide range in physical abilities.

As with most sports, your fitness will influence the boat you choose to sail. Australia's Bill Northam was his country's oldest Gold Medal winner at 59 when he skippered in the relatively sedate 5.5 metre class at the Tokyo Olympics. Such a feat is near impossible in today's smaller and more fitness-orientated Olympic classes. However, many small boat events for masters sailors have sprung up given the nature of the sport which mixes brain with brawn.

Sailing a classic can place high loads on the arm and shoulder muscles.

Factors that reduce blood pressure:
Regular exercise
Lower salt intake
Lower body fat levels
Relaxation
Lower fat diet

There are many resources that deal with Fitness in Masters sport and I refer you to those for good general information. For the sailor, there are a few specific concerns. Hiking generates very high blood pressure. Even though you may not be breathing especially hard when hiking, the heart may be struggling in the high-pressure fluid system that is trying to force blood through narrowed vessels. Therefore, you must devote yourself to gaining sufficient fitness before tackling a windy regatta.

In terms of muscle strength, there is usually a peak when you are around 30 years old and thereafter a slow decline. However, substantial strength is retained into later life, especially in those who remain active and this is important for everyday life as well as for your sailing performance.

Aerobic fitness will also gradually decline from the low to mid 30s. However, there are many examples of 30 and 40 year-olds who are world-beaters in endurance-based sports.

As you get older the physical concern that many people have is a reduced ability to recover from exercise, or, in fact, from any injury or general physical stress. Hormonal changes in the body are responsible for the slowed regeneration of the muscles. Alcohol post-race will also slow recovery.

Your maximum heart rate is thought to decrease with age, but it is difficult to give a simple prescription (e.g., heart rate) on which to base exercise intensity. The commonly given formula that says your maximum heart rate equals 220 minus you age is frequently inaccurate. Fitness testing at a gym or using the protocol outlined in this book can provide a good guide as to what level you're at.

Below is a simple case study for a master sailor's training.

Case Study 2 – Dougy

Subject:	40 years old, been sailing 20 years on and off.
Sailing History:	Experienced many different boats and crew positions. Now has settled into a Laser and races at club level, with the occasional larger competition.
Goals:	To keep enjoying sailing and win the club championship next season. Body weight is ok.
Sails:	1-2 days per week - Club racing at the weekend, plus the occasional after-work sailing and weekend regattas.

For **suppleness**, this subject undertakes 10-15 minutes of stretching after his gym and aerobic sessions and after sailing. He isn't getting any younger and still has a few niggling injuries, so needs to take care of his body.

To develop his **strength** for sheeting and adjusting the sail's controls, he completes two resistance-training sessions a week. One involves doing exercises for most of the body and he does it at the local gym (in about 45 min). The other he completes at home (in about 30 min), in a circuit-type format using a rope and pulley system (and some bricks!), a few pieces of shock cord and some floor space. He has had a bad back, so his sessions include 10 minutes of abdominal and lower back exercises, to stretch and strengthen the area.

Doug does two sessions a week devoted to developing his **stamina**. One depends on the weather - he cycles to work on either Wednesday or Friday - whichever it's not raining. The other is 20 minutes of hiking that he does in front of the TV. He has a mainsheet (loaded up via shock cord) on his hiking bench and pretends he is racing.

To keep his sailing **skills** sharp, Doug makes sure he fits in some non-competitive sailing sessions. During these, he can continue to hone his skills without the pressure of competition.

This subject is an avid reader of books on the **mental** side of competition. He has copies of Stuart Walker's "Tactics of small boat racing" and "Advanced Racing Tactics"!

Summary of average week's work	
Monday	Strength
Tuesday	Rest
Wednesday	Stamina (cycle) or Sail
Thursday	Strength
Friday	Stamina (hiking)
Saturday	Sail
Sunday	Rest

▶Comments

While this is Doug's basic exercise plan for each week, he knows that sometimes he won't have time to complete the nominated session; other times the wind may not be right for sailing. So, he keeps flexible (in his head), ready to adjust his weekly training plan at fairly short notice.

To make sure he improves his fitness, Doug will gradually increase the duration of his hiking sessions (by two minutes per week), plus increase the size of the weights he moves in the strength sessions. Two rest days are provided per week, to ensure the recovery he needs to work efficiently during the exercise sessions. The hiking bench is a great training tool that directly targets the muscle and energy systems used in sailing - a highly efficient way to improve his fitness for sailing.

▶▶ 18. LIFESTYLE FACTORS

Regular training should lead to a gradual increase in your sailing fitness and skill. However, little things can stop you and your body from getting the most out of your training.

You have to consider whether there might be some latent factor in your lifestyle that is having a minor but significant impact on your training. For example, a fellow sailor suffered from the so-called Chronic Fatigue Syndrome for more than a year. He tried many cures and eventually decided to have the mercury fillings removed from his teeth. It turned out that mercury might have leeched into his body from the fillings, depressing the immune system. It may have been a coincidence, but his health soon improved – little things may cause bigger problems.

Here are some examples of other latent factors and how they may cause a constant drain on the system, keeping you from reaching your potential:

- Bedding – too hard or soft? Too old? – This can affect the quality of your sleep and therefore mental and physical recovery.
- Suffering from any manageable allergies (eg, hay fever) – a house full of carpet can often harbour a lot more dust than one with bare floors.
- Time management – If you're going to do an Olympic campaign that can last 4 years or more you still can't waste time on things like daily travel (to school, work and training). Choose to live as close as possible to training (considering costs involved). The less time commuting the better.
- Physical potential – If you're not taller than, say 180cm, you'll have difficulty reaching the 95-100kg necessary to sail a Finn; conversely this may be too tall for a 470 skipper. These are obviously vital considerations to be made early when deciding which class of boat to sail. I know a girl who wanted to get stuck into an Olympic class but struggled to increase her weight for the Europe dinghy. She spent a couple of years in the class and was off the pace in windy conditions. She was a great size to steer a 470 and although it took a little convincing and effort to find a compatible crew, the change meant she could stop focusing on beefing up and start concentrating on sailing.
- Long-term injury – e.g., lower back soreness. Sitting in a chair all day at work will not help. You may like to invest in a Swiss ball. Sitting on a Swiss ball corrects the problem found in conventional seating of slump in the lower back. The curve of the Swiss ball adjusts to your body weight and helps tilt the pelvis gently forward, especially when we sit open legged. The advantage is that the angle between the thigh and the trunk is increased, thus reducing the hamstring muscles tendency to tip the pelvis backward. The slight instability of the Swiss ball also stimulates

Swiss ball – a big, sturdy blow up ball you can sit and do exercises on.

the sensory reflexes to tighten the abdominal muscles and activate the extensor muscles of the back. So, it is easier to maintain good posture. The body then learns a new behaviour pattern - dynamic sitting, reducing the problems associated with static sitting.
- Resources – Consider whether you will have access to the resources you will need to progress (eg, money, equipment and coaching). An important resource is a good training partner. He or she will provide the competition you need to extend your limits.
- Are you enjoying it? – Your motivation should be your own. If you enjoy sailboat racing for its inherent characteristics then you will be in a better frame of mind to analyse and take home the lessons from each race. However, if you're blinded by a focus on counting places and keeping score and are afraid of being beaten, you may not be so open to appreciating the little things that make the difference.

The above are all long-term factors that are of major significance when preparing for a lofty goal. Consider each carefully when you start to develop your grand plan and aim to live and train in an environment that facilitates your improvement.

Enjoying your sailing has an important role in your improvement.

▶▶ 19. ON-WATER TRAINING

▶ Training Drills

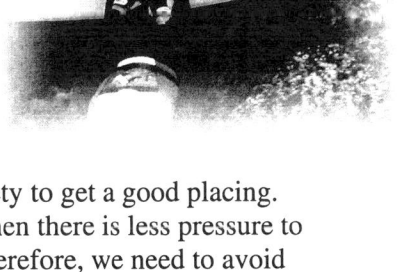

A desire to win rarely results in sailing well, but sailing well often results in winning.
– Dr. Stuart Walker

A race is not the best environment to learn and practice all the skills of sailing. There's too much pressure and anxiety to get a good placing. The mind and muscles learn things better when there is less pressure to perform and the outcome doesn't matter. Therefore, we need to avoid just racing all the time in order to practice sailing excellently. Then, as Stuart Walker suggests, when we are sailing better, winning comes naturally.

Rather than just 'go sailing' it is important to productively use the learning and training time you set for yourself. For this purpose there are endless types of training drills that isolate the different parts of a race that need to be improved.

Below is just a small sample of useful drills. They isolate specific parts of a race and allow you to concentrate on that part. You get dozens of races worth of starts, tacks and mark roundings in one session. Also, the emphasis is on personal improvement while downplaying competition. You can try new or different things and learn the results without suffering from the loss of confidence involved in 'losing'. In this sense you are really 'playing' sailing and discovering things with a child-like approach, but doing it in a very structured and purposeful manner.

These exercises can be done with or without a coach or other person present in a powerboat. If alone, the sailors should get together after each run-through to discuss the things that came out of the drill, such as why someone went ahead or behind or what technique worked best. Try four to five of the drills below in one two-hour on-water session for variety and to work on a range of sailing skills.

> Your heart rate during windy sailing can be as high as 190 beats/min with sustained rates of 160-170 bpm sailing upwind.
>
> Although breathing is not especially hard, these numbers show that there is high stress on the heart and blood pressure is extreme.
>
> Even in light winds, heart rate can rise to 130 or more in the starting sequence due to anxiety.

• Upwind Steering, Trim and Speed

Looking behind. Sailing upwind, turn and look at the horizon behind you rather than in front. Now you are forced to sail the boat more by feel. Remember to keep hiking and/or trapezing and steer and trim the sails according to gusts, lulls and shifts you feel in the breeze. Start to feel where the boat wants to go.

Steering with a rope. Tie a short rope or the end of your mainsheet around the end of your tiller and begin steering using the rope instead of the tiller extension. Now, you can only pull at the helm rather than push and pull. With weather helm, you can ease the rope to let the boat luff gently over waves and with gusts and then pull the rope to bear away smoothly over the back of waves.

Lasers straight-lining to test boat speed and height.

Try sailing for two minutes with the rope, then swap back to the tiller extension for one minute, aiming to keep steering as smoothly as you did with the rope (trim the sails too). Keep changing between rope and tiller extension until you get the hang of it or for 10 minutes. Gradually, your movements on the helm will decrease in magnitude causing less rudder drag as you begin to anticipate when to let the tiller go to leeward.

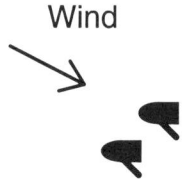

Wind

Lee-bowed (two boats). Too often people tack on your lee-bow but rarely do we practice coping with it. For this exercise, one boat starts with her bow approximately level with the skipper of the other boat and about two metres to windward. Then, the boats go at full speed, with the windward boat especially forced to concentrate on her speed and height to avoid the other's wind shadow. You soon find out that the size of the wind deflection off the sail(s) is greater in lighter winds, so a greater gap between the boats is necessary when it's light. Swap places once the windward boat falls back or gains height and gets to clear air.

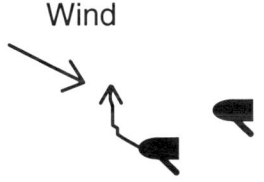

Judging tacking (two boats). Often you need to accurately judge when you can tack and cross a boat on your weather hip. In the above lee-bow exercise, most of the time the windward boat will fall back slowly. When she thinks there is sufficient room, the leeward boat should tack to cross the windward boat. This allows practice in judging how much room you need to tack and clear that windward boat. The windward boat should give feedback to the leeward boat as to the distance she crossed with, or if a collision would have occurred.

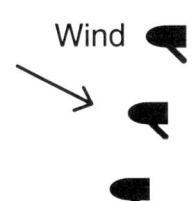

Boat speed and height (two or four boats). Otherwise known as two-boat tuning, this is where boats line up, close enough to be sailing in the same bit of wind, but far enough apart to be in clear air. When the boats are in position, it is probably best for someone to say 'go' and then all sail at absolute top speed for as long as possible to simulate what you would do off a start line in a race. You can go for a set period, for example, 5 to 10 minutes, or until there is a clear leader. Crews then stop and discuss what happened – maybe the sail trim or steering techniques varied a little between the boats. Start again or change positions to confirm the advantage was not just a one-off.

Speed differences in many one-design classes are small and take time to be seen, so persist until you are sure. This means being scientific as to what you attribute the speed or height differences – a slight wind shift or an abnormally large set of waves can affect only one boat and should be taken in account when deciding why you were slower or faster. Also, be observant for differences in the height the boats are sailing, as well as their speed forward. This is vital since extra height can really help off the start line and when being lee-bowed.

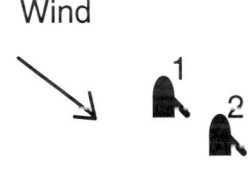

Two-on-one (three boats). Boats one and three (usually sailing upwind) are on the same team, trying to convert their positions into a one-two combination. As soon as a change in places occurs, the new one and three become teammates and the drill continues.

• General Handling

Crowded! (one or more boats). This exercise is done within a group of moored boats or inside a marina with boats, pylons, etc. all around. It is designed to simulate the crowded nature of large-fleet starts and races when you actually have few boats to work with.

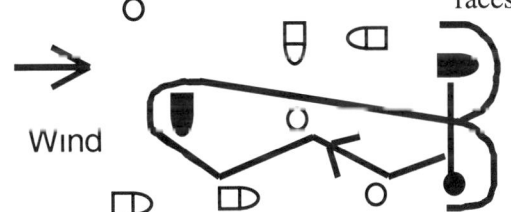

Pick out a short start line from amongst the boats/pylons and pick out a windward mark from any one of the number of boats/pylons that are suitable. After, say, a two-minute starting sequence, sail up around the top mark (not hitting anything along the way).

At the bottom of the run of this two-lap course you have the option of rounding the port mark to port or the starboard mark to starboard before heading back up to the windward mark for the final run to the finish. Do the course a couple of times before picking out a completely new start line and windward mark. This renews the novelty of the course, keeping it less familiar than the bottom of your boat!

Course layouts. Sometimes there are different course layouts at different regattas. Heard of the outer loop trapezoid, inner loop trapezoid, full-round trapezoid and windward/return triangle courses? Try these out in miniature – examining the different tactics and techniques that might apply as well as pressurising your boat-handling skills over the mini-courses. Use your own small buoys or pick out a suitable course from amongst moored boats or channel markers.

 Wind

Outer loop trapezoid   Inner loop trapezoid   Double-round trapezoid   Windward-return, triangle

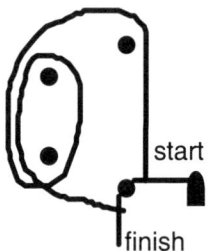 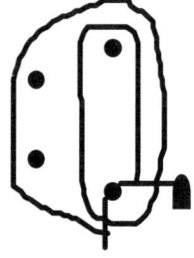 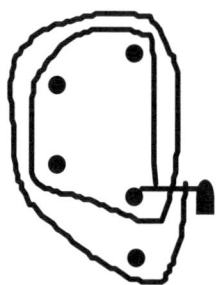 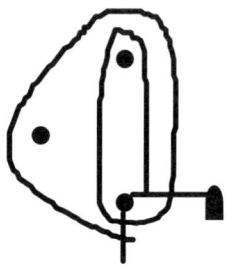

start / finish

- **Tacking**

Cross tacking (two boats). Sailing upwind, the drill starts with a gate start (one boat passing close behind the other). Then, every 20 or so metres the boats tack back toward each other again, crossing with port giving way to starboard if necessary. The tacks continue like this with the better tacker of the two gradually pulling ahead. Stop when a clear advantage has been gained. As the wind gets stronger, the distance between tacks should be increased slightly to give each crew time to set-up properly on the new tack.

Tacking 20 sec (one boat). This is similar to the cross-tacking exercise, but is done on your own, making it a self-discovery drill. You tack about every 20 seconds for, say, five minutes, choosing the least choppy water to tack in. You can apply specific aims to the exercise, such as delaying crossing the boat until the last possible moment, limiting or exaggerating the amount of helm you use or trying to roll or keep the boat as flat as possible when tacking. The objective is to learn how to exit the tack at the highest speed and height.

Good timing on this roll gybe means little speed is lost.

Covering upwind (two boats). The 'covered' boat starts close off the leeward stern of the covering boat. Then stopwatches start and the leeward boat has five minutes to get past the windward boat through repetitive tacking, dummy tacks, sailing faster and so on. Usually the drill starts with the leeward boat making an initial tack away to clear her air, followed by a covering tack by the windward boat and so on.

• Gybing

Just do them! After a long upwind effort, reach downwind, doing repeated gybes. The best technique changes slightly with the wind strength and usually involves a quick pump of the mainsheet or a tug on the vang assembly to help the mainsail come across. As your confidence improves, try gybing in stronger and stronger breezes. Try gybing without changing hands on the mainsheet and tiller extension; gybing when the boat is at its slowest ploughing into a wave, and at its fastest, surfing down a monster wave. Try to minimise the time the spinnaker is not full.

Timing is everything – crew movement across the boat; when to tug at the mainsheet; when and how much to steer; which part of the gust or wave – all need to be experimented with so that gradually the right combination is found for each set of wind and wave conditions.

Accelerate and sail high and fast off the start line.

• Starting Boat-Handling

Acceleration. Start your stopwatch with your bow just few metres behind a buoy (pretend the buoy is either the port or starboard end of a start line). Pretend the starting signal is when your watch reaches 20 seconds. Do what it takes to accelerate to cross the line at full speed and height at that 20-second mark. Sail fast upwind for 20 more seconds then come back and start again.

Find out the best way to accelerate your boat – should you sheet on gradually and slowly round up to close-hauled, or pull the sheet on hard and hike the boat flat straight away? The time to accelerate to full speed and the best way to accelerate will depend on the conditions.

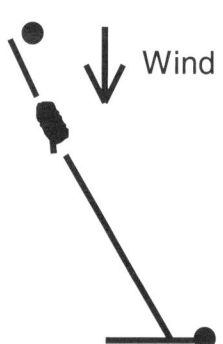

First 100m. Find a buoy to use as one end of the start line and a buoy about 100m away on your starboard-tack layline. Using, say, a 30 second count-down, start next to the buoy and sail as fast as possible to the 100m buoy, recording the time it takes to get there. As long as the wind conditions are relatively steady, this is a good drill for working on getting out of the blocks quickly and sailing the most important part of the race at full speed.

Good communication and coordination between skipper and crew are needed to get off the start line quickly.

Low-speed control. Park your bow almost touching a buoy and try to keep it within a metre of the buoy for as long as possible. Tack, luff, back the sail and steer forcefully to keep the bow in position.

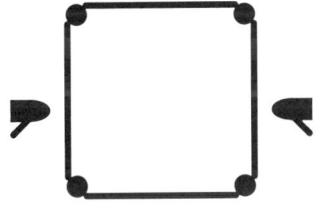

Forcing out (two boats). A square less than 40m wide is set. On a signal, the boats enter the square from either side. The aim is to legally force the other boat out of the box. This drill tests starting handling and rules knowledge.

Match racing starts (two boats). A five-minute signal is made. At four minutes to go the boats cross through the start line from windward to leeward starting from outside either end of the line. Each boat must cross through the line in this manner before she can start – usually the earlier the better (i.e., at the four minute mark). The boats then are free to gain the best possible start for themselves – at the expense of the other boat's start! The drill can stop when the boats cross the line to start, or the boats can continue sailing to a windward mark, which they round and run back through the line to finish. Boats should swap ends of the line for the next start.

The length of the line and its angle to the wind should be varied after a couple of run-throughs of the above starting exercises so that the crew can practice starting techniques which may better suit start lines of different biases and lengths.

• Mark Rounding Boat-Handling

Short-courses (one or more boats). A windward-leeward course can be set with the buoys only 20 – 50 m apart (depending on wind strength). Boats can start via a gate start or a start line can be set. Do two to three laps, adjusting all sail and boat controls as appropriate for each leg of the course. This is great practice in strong winds for getting around the buoys in the quickest possible time.

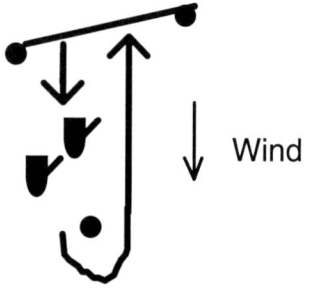

Leeward mark rounding (two – ten boats). From a running start off a line biased to the outside, sail to a bottom mark 30 to 80 m away. The aim is to get the best possible rounding, so an inside overlap or clear ahead is favoured. Finish at the start line.

• Reaching

Reaching speed (two to five boats). To test beam reaching speed, the boats usually have to line up slightly further apart than for upwind tuning. Then the leeward boat retains clear air for long enough to see who's fastest. Alternatively, try the timed reaching runs described below. In two-boat tuning while running, simply start side-by-side.

Timed reaching runs (one or two boats). A set of marks in a rectangular formation are needed, set perpendicular to the wind. The rectangle should be about 100m long and high enough to ensure there are no wind-shadow effects. The boats sail around either the windward or leeward set of marks only. A one-minute signal is given. Starting on a reach, boats pass to leeward of their mark and sail to their end mark and gybe. Then they aim to pass just to leeward of the start mark as quickly as possible. When the wind is steady, a single boat can do this exercise, timing the runs with a stopwatch, trying to beat her last time. This is a good exercise to test reaching speed since there is little chance of the bow-wave or wind-shadow of one boat affecting the other.

• Physical Fitness

Many of the above drills can be used with the aim of working on your physical fitness as well as sailing skills. However, note that it's best to learn new skills when you're fresh, so it may be best to leave these exercises until the end of an on-water session. Some of the more physically demanding on-water exercises were listed earlier in the section on Top Training Sessions.

49er sailors need to practice their boat handling to stay dry.

▶ Sample On Water Training Session

If you go on the water with a plan you are more likely to achieve the short-term goals you have in mind. With these stepping-stones, it's easier to make progress toward your long-term objective.

The session below will involve you performing most of the skills of sailing. However, on some days you may choose to work on just one particular skill. The contents of your on-water training should be modified according to the phases of your yearly plan or to target any weaknesses that come up. If you're a little slow (and couldn't we all do with a tad more speed!) you might devote whole sessions to working on your straight-line speed. With a regatta approaching, you could put more starts and short-course races into a session to hone-up your racing skills.

Cumulative Time (hr:min)	Drill
0:00	Sail to training area Warm-up hiking and sheeting - light effort Stretch muscles - 15 min
0:15	Looking behind drill - upwind - 5 min
0:20	Boat speed and height drill - 20 min
0:40	Lee-bowed drill - 10 min
0:50	Running speed - 15 min
1:05	Forcings-out drill - 10 min
1:15	Cross-tacking drill - 10 min
1:25	Gybing downwind - 5 min
1:30	Short courses - 4 races - 20 min
1:50	Sail in/warm-down and stretch - 10 min
2:00	Arrive beach

Following each session it's a good idea to write notes on what you've learnt each day in a logbook. Before a major regatta, look back through your notes as a reminder of what you've achieved in training. Things to note in your logbook include:

- Date, location, venue, weather conditions.
- Pre-start information and preparation.
- Goal(s) for the day.
- Sail, mast and other settings.
- Strategy, tactics and race path.
- Race result(s).
- Key errors and reasons why you passed boats or others passed you.
- Mental attitude and state of mind before going onto the water and during the race.
- Any problems with sleep or anxiety.
- Any distractions from work, family or financial problems.
- Your fitness and how well you stood up to the demands of sailing.
- Key areas to work on.
- Your strengths and weaknesses.
- Any 'local knowledge' you might have determined - current, geographic shifts, etc.

- Rule infringement situations.
- Information on the opposition.
- New boat handling techniques you have discovered.
- Any damage to your boat and equipment that needs fixing.
- Any physical injuries to you or your crew.

▶▶20. "LIKE RIDING A BIKE" - SAILING SKILLS

Sailing is made up of a plethora of specific skills. Whenever we move to body to perform a specific function on the boat, then that's a skill. But, they're not always easy to learn or perfect and this fact stops us sailing as well as we can.

Once a skill is learnt there comes a relatively permanent change in your head and body that makes it feel more normal to perform this skill again and again - just like riding a bike. The muscles develop a memory for movement - the strength needed, range of movement and timing of effort. The trick is getting the body and mind to learn and remember the required sequence of movements as quickly and easily as possible. Since sailing requires that a large number of individual skills be learnt - tacking, gybing, steering upwind, light winds, big waves and so on - it's necessary to improve and refine your skills with as little fuss as possible.

There are a number of techniques we can use to enhance skill learning, for example: using cue words; breaking a complex skill down into simpler parts; doing repetitive practice.

▶ Cue Words

Say to yourself as you go through a tack in your mind or on the water:

Roll
Dash
HIKE
Trim

When you've been sailing along in a straight line for a while, the mind can start to wander just at a time you need to focus on a specific skill, like an upcoming tack. Using cue words can help to direct your attention to key elements of the skill. To focus on the main elements of tacking, you can enlist the cue words Roll, Dash, Hike and Trim. Murmur to yourself "Roll" as you prepare to tack to aware yourself of the trim of the hull, to help it steer up into the wind with little forceful rudder movement. "Dash" - rush to the other side once you pass head to wind to minimize the time the sail luffs. Then you need to "Hike" the boat flat to power up and accelerate out of the tack. Finally, think how to re-"Trim" the hull and sails for optimal upwind performance.

▶ Breaking Down Skills

If you have trouble getting all the movements of tacking (or any other skill) flowing well together, try breaking the skill down and practice one part at a time. There are many parts you can single-out – preparing to go about, the movement across the boat, the exit from the tack and re-gaining speed. You could just practice exiting the tack and getting up to full speed. Focusing on the exit to the tack makes it easier to get it right without worrying about the rest of the tack. You should always finish this part-practice by doing a few complete tacks, putting all the pre-learned movements together.

▶ Practice

This may remind you of the P-sayings: "practice makes perfect", or to be proper; "perfect practice makes perfect". It's important to learn a skill correctly the first time to avoid bad habits developing. Repetitive practice of the one skill can get monotonous but it helps you solidify the movement patterns within your body and mind.

It's like cutting a new groove in a record. As long as you keep scratching along the same path, the grove will get deeper and the more likely the needle will fall into that path the next time you need that skill. If you practice a skill poorly you'll be scratching a number of shallow grooves in the record. The next time you go to play that song (skill) you'll get a mix of wanted and unwanted performances.

▶ Highly Skilled?

There are two main ways of determining whether you have a skill down pat. First, whether you can do it to a high degree of proficiency. Second, how consistently you can repeat the same skill.

Really good sailors seem to have all the time in the world when they are in tight situations. They react quickly, but look unhurried in a series of smooth, efficient movements. They can repeat the skill perfectly, yet make modifications to deal with novel demands - such as to tack through a bad set of waves. Contrast this with the novice who always seems rushed, unorganised and unclear as to what to do next. Sometimes they will do a good- looking tack or gybe but will not be able to repeat it on demand. The highly skilled sailor has the benefit of having that groove deeply cut into his or her record.

▶ Too Similar Skills

Take two sports - tennis and squash - similar in skills yet with some important differences. In squash, the ball comes back faster than tennis, so the players only have time to swing the racquet at the small rubber ball using a lot of wrist movement and relatively little movement of the rest of the arm or body. In tennis, the players often have enough time to get the racket head moving by rotation of the trunk, shoulder and arm in a specific sequence.

Play squash for a while then switch to tennis and you find yourself swatting at the ball using your wrist and delivering strokes which lack enough power to get the bigger tennis ball back over the net. In short, it is quite difficult to learn or perform a skill that is very similar in its movement pattern to one you have mastered. So, if you want to be a top tennis player and like to play some other sport as a hobby, try something less similar than squash!

The same goes for sailing. The above can be true when you switch classes of sailboat, especially for the feel of a boat you get when steering. Most boats feel different to steer - even two one-designs - and getting the feel of a new boat takes time to get your steering accurate enough to sail fast through waves, shifts and gusts. Therefore, you should allow a reasonable period to get the feel of a different class before giving it up as too hard. If you often sail different classes of boat, the other implication is not to spend too much time in one class before an important championship in another.

All skill – light winds require careful sail trimming and boat balance.

In summary, to get the best out of your practice:
- Introduce simplest skills first
- Gradually add more intensity and demand until the skill can be performed in the most difficult of situations.
- Use cue words and imagery to get the timing right.
- Remember that interest and enthusiasm are the parents of skill.

▶▶FINALLY

The exercises and ideas in this book are not just for seriously competitive sailors. You may sail mostly in local competitions and go to a bigger regatta once a year to see where you're at; you'll be better than last year if you're fitter and can handle the boat well. The reassurance you get from sailing better will, I hope, help you achieve whatever your goals may be. Get out on the water as much as you can and great sailing!

▶▶ SAILING LIBRARY

Bourke, G., & Rothfield, M. (1993). *Championship Laser Racing.* Fernhurst, Great Britain.
Glenn's secrets on every aspect of Laser racing, including physical training. A must for both Laser club racers and championship competitors and of interest to all sailors.

Blackburn, M.J. (1994). Physiological responses to 90 minutes of simulated dinghy sailing. *Journal of Sports Sciences.* 12:383-390.
The scientific report on my study on hiking.

Blackburn, M., Hubinger, L. (1994). *Physical characteristics of and training programs for dinghy sailors (coaches' report).* Unpublished report to the Australian Sports Commission.
A group of small boat sailors were given a training program to follow and completed fitness tests before and after eight weeks of specific training. Report on the study available from the Australian Sports Commission.

Elvstrom, P. (1964). *Expert Dinghy Racing.* Adlard Coles Ltd., London.
The winner of four Olympic gold medals explains his training methods that were revolutionary at the time.

Gallwey, W.T. (1976). *Inner tennis: Playing the game.* Random House, New York.
"A tennis player first confronts the Inner Game when he discovers that there is an opponent inside his own head more formidable than the one across the net. He then realises that the greatest difficulty in returning a deep backhand lies not in the speed and placement of the ball itself, but in his mind's reaction to that ball: his own thinking makes the shot more difficult than it really is. Further, he becomes aware that these same mental obstacles which keep him from playing his best tennis also prevent him from living his best life." Despite its focus on tennis, it is a great book that can help you improve your feel for and mental approach to sailing.

Hoyt, G.(1971). *Go for the Gold.* Nautical, England.
A no-nonsense account of the mental style needed to win.

Orlick, T. (1990). *In Pursuit of Excellence.* Leisure Press, Illinois.
An easy read by a sports psychologist with great practical revelations and tips in areas like mental imagery, focusing, goal setting, working with coaches, self-confidence and control.

LaserCoach 2000. (1999). Interactive training CD ROM. SailCoach Associates.
A great multimedia resource that includes many video clips of Laser skills.

Spurway, N. (1993). Sailing sport medicine. *Medical Science Research,* 21(23).
Special issue devoted to sailing physiology and injury.

Tan, B. (2000). *The complete introduction to Laser racing.* Singapore Sports Council.
A recent well-written book on the Laser.

Twiname, E., Foster, C. (1993). *Sail, Race and Win.* Adlard Coles Nautical, London.
Aims to move you up the fleet by coaching yourself. Helps you with plans of attack as well as tips on physical and mental fitness. Great practical suggestions and insights.

Walker, S.H. (1976). *Advanced Racing Tactics.* Angus & Robertson, Australia.
Described as the 'Bible' to sail racing, ART is a solid description of most reliable tactical and strategical principles. Stuart Walker's other books, Positioning - The Logic of Sailboat Racing (1991) and The Tactics of Small Boat Racing (1966), are also good, but repeat each other in a few places. Winning - the Psychology of Competition (1980) can be heavy reading at times but otherwise is a good nuts and bolts review of the mental factors that aid or hinder winning.

▶▶ APPENDIX: GYM EXERCISES

| Abdominal | Strong abdominal muscles are important for all-round fitness and strength as they provide the muscular link between the upper and lower body |

Sit-up
With knees bent, perform normal full sit-ups. Ensure the motion is as smooth as possible. The hands can be unclasped behind the head or touching the forehead. Avoid swinging your arms to help lift the trunk.

Variation:
Twisting sit-up - With hands touching ears, sit-up and twist so that your elbows approach you knees alternately.

Side raise (elevated)
Mount a back extension machine or a Swiss ball so that one hip is pointing down, the other up. Start with your trunk parallel to the floor. Bend down and back up past horizontal. Keep your shoulders in line with your hips. Your hands can be held against the chest or behind the head to make the exercise easier or harder, respectively.

Crunch
A partial sit-up in which you lift the trunk, but not the lower back, off the floor. Therefore, the hip flexor muscles are not involved.

Variation:
Twisting Crunch - With your hands behind your head, your elbows will twist towards your opposite knee.

Hiking sit-up
Mount back extension machine or Swiss ball as if hiking. Now perform normal sit-ups. However, strictly avoid leaning further back than horizontal.

Variation:
Hiking throw downs: Start roughly in a hiking position on a hiking bench, back extension apparatus or Swiss ball in a gym. Raise the trunk up from a hiking position. A training partner stands behind you, catching your shoulders as they are raised then throwing then down. The training partner should vary height from which the shoulders are thrown down.

Hiking medicine ball throw
Mount a back extension machine or Swiss ball as if hiking. If you're on a Swiss ball, the feet will need to be held by a heavy weight. With medicine ball in hand, throw and catch the ball in alternate hands. Throw the ball to different heights and to the side to load the muscles over a wide range. A hard exercise when a heavier ball is used.

Toe touch
Start by lying on your back with your feet on the ground, knees at 90 degrees. Curl up so that your shoulders are off the ground. Rotate alternately to each side, touching each ankle with your fingers.

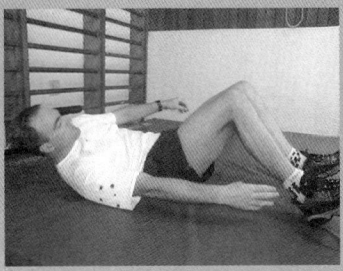

Side crunch
Lying on your side on the floor, knees bent, slide your upper arm and hand down your thigh by side-flexion of the trunk. Repeat on other side.

Medicine ball side passes
Sit on the ground (either next to a solid wall or a training partner). Then, throw a medicine ball strongly against the wall and catch. Change sides after the set number of repetitions. Can also be done standing.

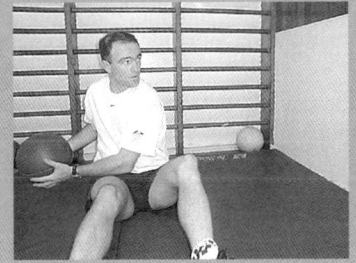 

Crucifix
Start by lying on your back with your arms extended straight out to the sides (like a "T"). Legs should be pointing to the ceiling. Lower the legs to one side (feet together). Then, up again and lower them on the other side. Your shoulders should remain on the floor at all times.

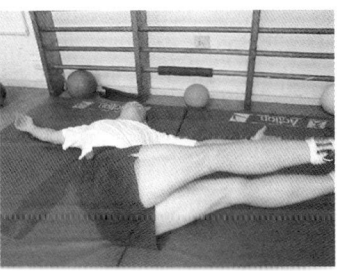

Reverse sit-up
Lay flat on ground, knees slightly bent. Lift both feet up, and well over your head and lower to just above the ground.

Single leg raise

Slow and controlled: Lie on floor. First, pull stomach to floor to flatten back. While keeping the lower back in contact with the floor slowly lift one leg straight to 45 degrees and lower. Repeat with other leg, all the time making sure your lower back is flat against the floor.

Variations:
1. Double leg raise - Lift both legs at once, making for a harder exercise. Maybe you will start your repetitions with double leg raises then switch to single leg as you get tired.
2. Leg raises/throw downs: Lying face up on an incline bench, hands clasping its top, raise your straight legs hard and fast. A training partner stands at your feet, catching them as they are raised, then throwing them down. The training partner should vary height from which the feet are thrown down.

V-sits

Lay flat on the floor. Do a dual-leg straight leg raise and hold at about 60 degrees. Now, perform normal crunch. A difficult exercise.

Hanging knee raise

Use one of two suitable apparatus at the gym (one where the elbows rest on the pads, holding the body vertical and off the ground or a simple hanging bar against a wall). Holding the abdominal muscles tight, lift your knees to near your chest and lower.

Variations:
1. Straight-legged - For added difficulty.
2. Medicine ball - Place between your bent knees for extra resistance

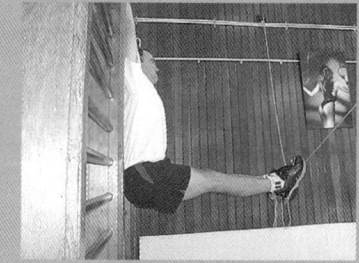

Hanging knee raise (left), straight-leg raise (right)

Swiss Ball
These exercises will add a little more physical instability plus variety to your program.

Prone alt. arm & leg

Lay prone on a Swiss ball, stomach roughly in the center of the ball and your hands and feet spread on the ground. Raise your opposite leg and arm above ball height and then lower. Repeat with your opposite leg and arm.

Seated single leg
Sit on the ball with your feet flat on the floor. Tighten your abdominal muscles (suck your stomach in). Lift one leg and hold for 10 sec, trying not to let the ball wobble or adjust your center of gravity. Repeat with other leg.

Prone hand walk
Lay with your chest on a Swiss ball, feet on floor. Then, roll forward so that your hands contact floor (and feet lift up) and walk forward on your hands so that your feet end up on top of the ball. 'Walk' back to the starting position. All the time, keep your stomach sucked in and stay on the ball!

Side bend in side lying
Lay on the floor on your side with your feet up on a Swiss ball. While leaning on your lower elbow and using your upper hand to balance, lift your whole body off the floor. Raise and lower your hip area, so that your body does side bends in both directions, up and down. A tough exercise.

 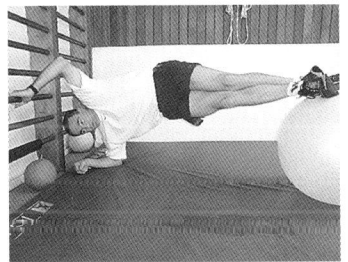

Swiss prone single-leg off
Start in full push-up position - toes on ball, hands shoulder width apart on ground. Slowly take one foot off the ball and move that leg out to the side and return it over a 5 sec period. Repeat on other side. Keep body horizontal.

Russian twist
Perform half a sit-up and then stop. Twist trunk fully to each side alternately. A weight can be used to add resistance.

Variation:
Hiking twist - Get in a hiking position on a back extension machine or on a Swiss ball. Twist your trunk fully to each side with a medicine ball in hand.

Forearm plank

Lay face down on a mat. Support your body by your elbows and toes. Hold that position, body as flat as possible, for 10 sec. Then 10s rest. Repeat for 2 min. Of course, you can alter the work:rest interval to suit.

Chest and triceps

Building up the chest is not usually a prime concern for sailors. However, these exercise are valuable to help balance the body, develop muscles for handling, say, a spinnaker pole, and will contribute to weight gain, where needed.

Push-ups

Lay prone on floor, hands shoulder-width apart and toes pointing to ground. Keeping your body and head in line, extend the arms fully and then lower your chest to the floor.

Variations:
1. Knees on floor - An easier alternative.
2. Feet elevated - More difficult. The feet go on a bench.
3. Feet on Swiss ball - Use a Swiss ball under your feet or knees for added stability training.
4. Push against wall - Standing, hands on wall, feet one meter back from the wall. Allows a greater number of repetitions to be done by those who are not yet as strong.

  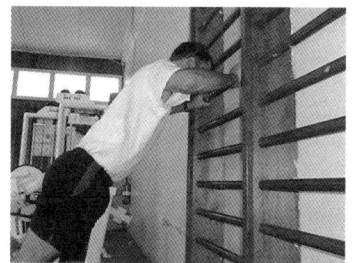

Feet on Swiss ball (left), push-ups against wall

Bench press (bar or dumbbell)

Use a flat bench plus a barbell or dumb-bells. Start with your hands slightly wider than shoulder width apart. Lower the weight slowly to just above your chest and push up strongly. Use a spotter for heavy weights. Keep your feet on the floor and your lower back against the bench.

Variations:
1. Decline - Using a decline bench results in slightly different muscle usage (ie, lower pectorals).
2. Dumbbells - (one weight in each hand) help develop each arm in isolation - useful if one arm is weaker.
3. Incline - Places more stress on your deltoids as well as chest muscles.

Bench press - dumbbells (above left), incline dumbbells (right)

Dips

Lift yourself off the floor, hands about shoulder width apart. Slowly lower until your elbows are bent about 90 degrees and push up strongly. As you get tired, exercise through a smaller range of motion or push off the floor.

Legs

It is important to develop good leg strength to have good hiking endurance. Building up these large muscles can also help greatly when you're trying to gain weight.

Leg extension

Sit in the machine with your ankles against the pad(s). Extend the legs fully, lower most of the way and extend again.

Variations:
1. Limit range of movement - Move your lower legs through only the last 15-20 degrees, similar to hiking.
2. Single leg - Use a weight less than 1/2 of your double-leg weight.

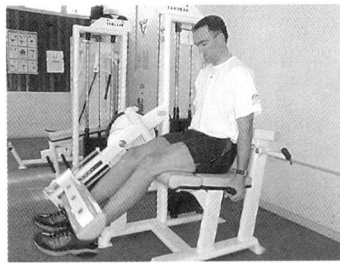

Leg press

Adjust the seat so that your knees are bent at 90 degrees in the starting position. Push out strongly and ease the load back.

Variations:
1. Limit range of movement - Move your legs through only the last 15-20 degrees, similar to hiking.
2. Single leg - Use a weight less than 1/2 of your double-leg weight.

Squats

Ideally, you will receive supervision when learning this exercise.
Move under the bar so that the muscles on the back and top of the shoulders contact the bar. Grasp the bar wider than shoulder width. Move the feet directly under the center of the weight. Lift the bar and set your footing - toes pointing slightly outward, feet almost shoulder width apart. Bend at your knees and slightly at the waist. Aim to keep your knees over the toes; head up; shoulders back; chest high. Lower to no more than 90 degrees at the knees. Drive the bar back up. Pause slightly between repetitions to ensure you are balanced.

Variations:
1. Split squat - With the bar on your shoulders, step forward about 50cm with one foot and regain your balance there. Carefully lower the weight by bending at both knees and drive back up. This exercise tests your balance a little more and requires more force from the front leg. Change legs after the set number of repetitions.
2. Smith machine - This can be used when learning. The bar is joined to tracks on either end and the bar runs up and down these tracks, adding to the safety of the exercise. The bar can be 'locked off' if you cannot lift it.
3. Dumbbells - If you have neck or shoulder problems, you can still perform squats with weights held in each hand. A lesser total weight will be used compared to a barbell squat.

Squat on Smith Machine (above left), dumbbell split squat (right)

Step-ups
With a bench or box about 40 cm high in front of you and dumbbells in each hand, step up one leg at a time and then down, same leg first. Change the lead leg over after the set number of repetitions.

Hiking leg extensions
Sitting in a hiking position on a back-extension machine or on a Swiss ball, extend the legs through the last few degrees possible and release. Lean back to add resistance.

Toe curls
To strengthen the ankle muscles, sit on the floor with the toes under a pair of dumbbells. You may need to put something under your heels to get a full range of motion. Flex the toes up and down (balancing the weight is difficult at first). A barbell can also be used.

Upper back & biceps
The muscles involved in these exercises are responsible for your sheeting or pumping power and endurance.

Lat pull-down
With trunk upright, pull the bar solidly down to your chin (being careful not to hit it!) and slowly ease it up again.

Variations:
1. U-bar - the hands are closer together, placing different strain on the biceps and latisimus muscles.
2. Behind neck - the bar can be brought down to the back of the neck, but be careful to not hit the vertebra.
3. Leaning back - lean the trunk back to about 45 degrees and pull the bar down to the chest.
4. Towel - Wrap a towel around the bar and grip it strongly with both hands. Good for developing the forearms as well as back/biceps.

Behind neck (far lower left), leaning back (above left), towel (right)

Chin-ups

Grasp the high bar at about shoulder width, palms forward. Pull the body upward and lower slowly to a straight-arm position.

Variations:
1. Towel/rope - A towel or thick rope can be thrown over the bar and used for chin-ups.
2. Assisted - the feet should be kicked up behind you and toes placed on a stool. This slightly lessens the difficulty, allowing more repetitions to be performed.
3. Weighted - For the strongest! A medicine ball can be held between the knees or feet for extra resistance.
4. Iron Cross - In the starting position, raise the legs to the horizontal and then begin your chin-ups, maintaining this leg position. An advanced exercise.

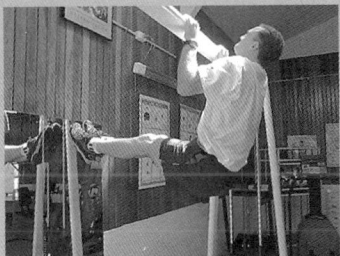

Clockwise from top left: Chin-up with towel; assisted chin-up; weighted chin-up; iron cross chin-up.

Seated row

Sit with legs comfortably in front. Keeping back stable, pull the handles strongly toward the stomach. Squeeze the shoulder blades together at the end of the movement

Variations:
1. 1-arm - Complete the rowing movement with one arm, being careful not to overload one side of the body.
2. Towel - Wrap a towel around the handle to develop your handgrip at the same time.
3. Scapular retraction - A shorter-range movement. Keeping the arms roughly straight, squeeze the shoulder blades (scapular) together firmly and then let the shoulders go forward again.

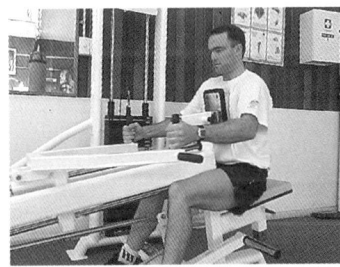
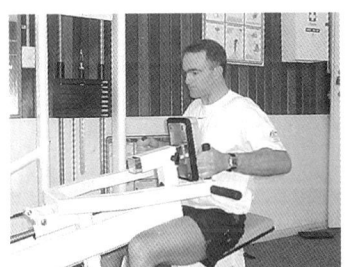

Body-weight pull-ups

Lie under a bar and use a bench, Swiss ball or similar to support the feet. With hands roughly shoulder width apart, pull the chest up to touch the bar and lower. Can also be done by lying on the floor and using a table.

High bench row
Lie face-down on a high bench with barbell or dumbbells at hand's length. Grasp the bar and pull it strongly upward to touch the underside of the bench. Lower slowly.

1-arm dumbbell row
With one hand and knee resting on a bench, pull a dumbbell up to the ribs and lower carefully. Keep the trunk flat and use only the arm and shoulder to move the weight.

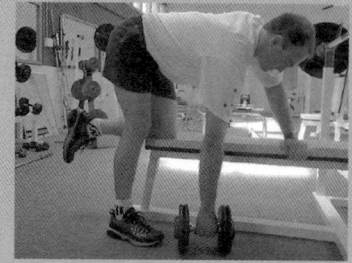 

Upright row
Pull a barbell up to near your chin, aiming to keep your elbows level. Your legs should be comfortably bent. Avoid swinging the trunk.

Rowing machine - sheeting
A rowing machine offers and alternative form of the 1-arm row. Simply pull the handle to the side of the stomach and release. Keep the shoulder low. You might like to pretend that your are 'elbowing' a punching bag behind you.

Bent-over lateral raise
Sitting on the end of a bench, grab the relatively light weights behind your legs and drive the back of the hands toward the ceiling, keeping the back stable. Your elbows should just pass the level of your back before lowering.

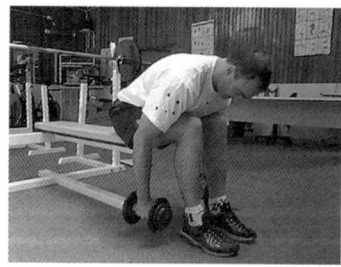 

Bicep curl

With your feet comfortably apart and barbell in hand, try to lock your elbows into your side. Pull the bar upward in a smooth arc and slowly lower. Avoid swinging the body.

Variations:
1. Dumbbell - The same exercise can be done with dumbbells. In that case, you can flex each arm alternately. This exercise can be done sitting, but I think you should avoid doing an incline bicep curl (where you lay 45 degrees back against a incline bench) as it may damage the shoulder joint when the weight is lowered.
2. Hammer Curl - very similar to the above, except the dumbbells are held like a hammer. This grip is more like that used when sailing.
3. Cable curl - Bicep curls can also be done using a weight stack. You stand near the weights and curl the bar upward in the normal fashion. You will notice that, rather than getting easier at the top, the level of resistance remains the same throughout the movement.

Hammer curls (above left), cable curl (right)

Lower back

The muscles being worked in these exercises are important for stabilizing the spine and so will help in the prevention of lower back problems.

Back extension

Bend over the back extension machine or Swiss ball (with feet anchored), head down. Slowly raise your trunk to in line with the legs, not above, and lower.
Too easy? - A light weight can be held to your chest.

Variations:
1. Swimming back extension - Start with body straight, hands touching your bottom. Swing one hand out above the head, then the other. Swing your arms back in the same order. A lightweight can be held in your hands.
2. With rotation - with your hands behind your head, slowly lower your trunk and rotate so that your right elbow would touch your left knee if you were standing. Uncoil back to the start position.

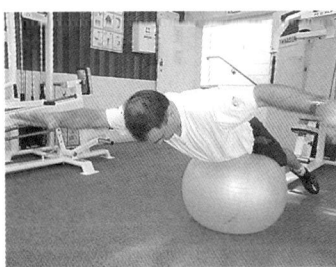

Swimming back extension

Reverse back extension

Use the back extension machine (or similar) but mount it the other way around so that your legs can be raised and lowered.

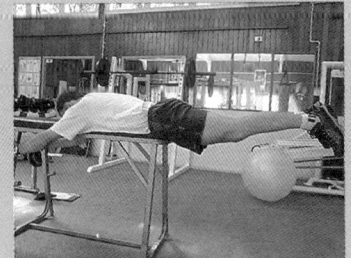

Superman
Lay prone on the floor, arms extended above your head and then lift your chest and legs off floor - like superman flying!

Shoulders

These exercises mainly work the large deltoid and other muscles that stabilize and move the arm.

3-way shoulder work
Lay on a high bench with a couple of relatively light weights in each hand. First you will do repetitions forward, then to the side, then to the rear. The hands should reach bench height at the top of each rep.

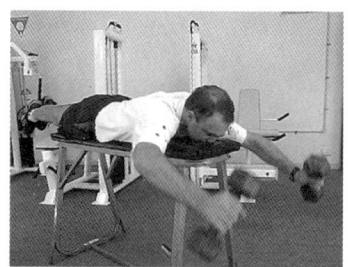
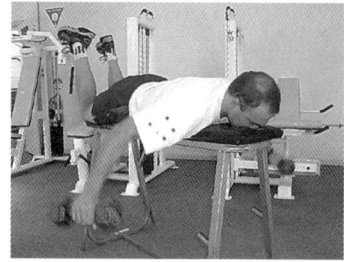
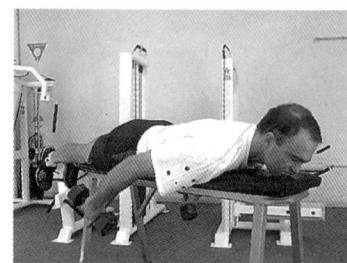

Shoulder work: forward (far left), lateral (above left) and backward (right)

Curl and press
Stand comfortably with dumbbells in each hand. Alternatively, with each hand, you will do a bicep curl immediately followed by a military press. Lower the same way.

Military press
Stand comfortably, knees slightly bent, with dumbbells in each hand at shoulder height. Push the weights skyward and lower. When the weights are pushed up, your hands should remain in line with the feet to maintain your balance.

Lateral raises
Stand comfortably with dumbbells in each hand. Pretend you're a bird and start flapping your wings. Your arms should reach horizontal before slowly lowering. Use a lighter weight if you can't reach the horizontal.

Abdominal stability

These exercises will help improve your control of your abdominal muscles. Once the abdominal muscles are developed sufficiently to provide a strong and stable core to your body, the more efficient the movements of your trunk and legs can be. These exercises can be done, say, after waking in the morning, three times a week.

Stretched out stomach suck

Lay on the floor with legs straight out in front. Hands raised up and pointing to the ceiling. Then, tighten your abdominals and push your belly button to the floor, flattening your lower back. Slowly lower your arms until they touch the floor over your head. Then raise arms until they point up towards the ceiling. Repeat 10 times.

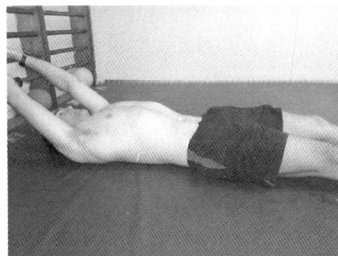

Controlled single-leg half-squat

Stand on one leg and bend the other leg up behind you. Then, squat on the standing leg so that your knee moves forward over the big toe. Down count = 2 seconds. Hold at bottom for 1 sec and return to start. To stop the hip dropping out to the side, tighten the gluteals on the standing leg throughout the movement. Tighten abdominals to stop 'hip drop' as well. Repeat 10 times with each leg.

Side leg raises

Lay on your side with legs straight. Then, raise and lower the top leg, keeping it straight. Repeat 10 times with each leg.

Bent leg raise

Lay on your back with knees bent and feet flat on floor. Tighten your abdominals and push your belly button to the floor, flattening your lower back. Then, slowly lift one leg off the floor 10cm and hold for 10 sec. Maintain abdominal control and don't allow your lower back to arch off the floor. Lower this leg back to the floor and repeat with other leg. Repeat 10 times with each leg.

Bad form: Back not flat to floor